GW00455559

Waiting for God:

From Trauma to Healing

John O'Brien OFM

© John O'Brien OFM 2015

For Susanna Stachura
gentil donna

Love is stronger than death

The deepest darkness is dispelled
by even a single ray of light
(Thomas of Celano, Second Life of St. Francis)

Contents

Abbreviations

GL: Theological Aesthetics (7 vols)

TD: Theodrama (5 vols)

TDNT: Theological Dictionary of the New Testament

TL: Theologic (3 vols)

Introduction

Trauma is the pain that never goes away. It emerges in dreams and as a reaction to a new trauma or stimulus. The pain can be destructive and overwhelming. This book is an attempt to be with the person in pain. I also involves a looking at Jesus. Hans Urs Von Balthasar and Adrienne Von Speyr spoke about the suffering of Jesus in the loneliness of his death and descent into Hell. Von Balthasar composed a work of theology called Theo-drama (5 vols - TD in the text). He uses the analogy of theatre to develop his theo-drama. There is a healing effect of seeing Jesus sharing our pain and asking him to bring light into our darkness. I conclude the work by looking at Samuel Beckett's 'Waiting for Godot'. He catches the pain of much of people's loneliness and dislocation - that feeling of not belonging. There is a cathartic effect in looking on Vladimir and Estragon. By analogy how much there is in being one with Jesus as the light of the resurrection begins to break in.

Chapter One

Can You See the Real "Me"?
Sometimes I Can't:-

'I went back to the doctor,
To get another shrink,
I sit and tell him about my weekend,
But he never betrays what he thinks.

Can you see the real me, doctor?

I went back to my mother
I said, "I'm crazy, Ma, help me."
She said "I know how it feels, son,
'Cause it runs in the family."
Can you see the real me, mother?'

('The Real Me', 1973 - The Who)

St. Francis (+1226), in his transformation into the life of Jesus by the Holy Spirit, showed a universal compassion for all of God's people and creatures - indeed for the whole of creation. This is the picture of St. Francis we find attractive. He lived in the spirit of God's love and radiated that love to others. He knew he was loved in God by the power of the Holy Spirit and those who came in contact with him experienced the radiance of that love.

Yet back in his youth could such a change be seen? In 1201, at the age of 19, Francis outfitted himself as a knight to join in the war against Assisi's rival, Perugia. After a humiliating defeat, Francis spent nearly a year as a prisoner while his father raised the money to pay his ransom. In 1205 he tried again to be a knight, he realised his call was elsewhere. Uncertain and pensive he returned to Assisi where his initial depression grew and became a full crisis. He felt a longing for human understanding which was denied him but at the same time opened the door for God to enter his life. He began to pray in lonely places and came to know the love of God revealed in Jesus, the Word of God made flesh (Jn 1:14). The road to his transformation had begun.

In his admonitions he tells us: "Try to realise the dignity God has conferred on you. He created you and formed your body in the image of his beloved Son, and your soul in his own likeness" (cf Gen 1:26), (Admonition 5) and in admonition 20 he tells us "What a man is before God, that he is and no more". We are children of God and beloved of him. We are accepted, loved and forgiven – it takes courage to accept this acceptance. The reason it takes courage is because through trauma and abuse many of us have learned not to accept ourselves. There are many who carry a deep wound that does not go away. There are many broken people among us and their pain and loneliness are very real. They are caught in a kind of twilight world where they cannot fully grasp their dignity as human beings. My experience of abuse and rejection has made this world known to me.

The Real Me:

The search of an identity, 'who am I', is a subject that artists, writers and musicians have put to the centre of their art. The Who's 1973 album Quadrophenia is one such effort that appeals to me. The hero James Michael Cooper (Jimmy for short) is first shown on a rock in the middle of a thunderstorm. He reflects on his very dark past up to that while the waves crash against the rocks. He screams out: "Can you see the real me? Can ya? CAN YA?" ("I am the Sea"). Jimmy's past begins to unfold in front of him and he recalls all the efforts different people made to understand him – his mother, the psychiatrist and preacher – all to no avail ("The Real Me"). He does not belong in his neighbourhood – nobody understands him there. He has a mental disorder called 'quadrophenia' – anybody can be schizophrenic, but Jimmy is quadrophenic. The story goes through Jimmy's seeking for belonging with the Mod group and his eventual disappointment and loneliness. At the end of the piece Jimmy gets a bottle of gin and begins to rage on with every weakness he sees and hates. Jimmy begins to see that he has to come to peace from within. He embraces the rain running over him and feels overjoyed, free and very spiritual, washing away the pain and bringing peace to his soul. In the end, Jimmy notes, love, no matter how fleeting or temporary it is, is a goal worth seeking and life is empty without it. This is expressed in the song "Love, Reign O'er Me".

> 'Only love can make it rain
> The way the beach is kissed by the sea
> Only love can make it rain
> Like the sweat of lovers layin' in the fields.
> Love, reign o'er me,
> Love, reign o'er me,
> rain on me, rain on me.'

Jimmy will go back and still struggle but now he will approach things differently. He has been touched in however an imperfect manner by love and he has a sense of his value as a person.

The Living Flame of Love:

God's Spirit which hovered over the waters or abyss at creation (Gen 1:1) is ever active. He is love and every so often we get glimpses of his action. The original Greek word for spirit, pneuma, translates the Hebrew word 'ruach'. It means 'wind' or 'breath'. The Hebrew mind did not know of such a thing as air, so 'ruach' refers to the dynamic movement, the energy generated by the passage of air. The wind is an energy that can set things in motion. This 'ruach' is the breath of the creator in which all things come to be. In the Old Testament we can say that the prophets and the great ones pray in the Holy Spirit.

In the first letter of St. John we read: "Think of the love that the Father has lavished on us, by letting us be called God's children and that is what we are" (1 Jn 3:1). St. Paul says that we received the spirit of being children, and the spirit "makes us cry out 'Abba: Father'" (Rom 8:16). This is where our dignity lies and even in the depths of distress teaching that we are the beloved of God. The thin view, the dim realisation that we are loved helps us live with the now in which for many of us the truth of what is said might be immediately self-evident.

It is hard to speak of the Spirit of love. Hans Urs Von Balthasar says: "This Spirit is breath, not a full outline, and therefore he wishes to breathe through us, not to present himself to us as an object; he does not wish to be seen but to be the seeing eye of grace in us and he is little concerned about whether we pray to him, provided we pray with him, "Abba, Father," provided we consent to his unutterable groaning in the depths of our soul." (The Unknown Lying Beyond the Word, p.111). Later on in another essay he says: "Thus the Holy Spirit appears (first) essentially as the common fruit of the Father and the Son which (secondly) can become autonomous in relation to them (the result is sent), and further (thirdly) as the gift of God to the world...." (The Holy Spirit as Love, p.125). He is the love that breaks through our darkness and through love leads us to life with God.

For Von Balthasar Christ is the proper object of our vision. The Holy Spirit remains hidden in revealing the love of God revealed in Jesus. The Holy Spirt leads us to participate in God's being in the world. To understand God's revelation is to participate in it.

The Spirit as Interpreter:

It is through Jesus' obedience in life and in death that God's love is revealed. This love is identical with the divine life itself. The Spirit's interpretation consists in making Jesus present to us, or even making us present to Jesus. The Spirit tries to make manifest the Word of the Father in all its fullness to the world. Until the Word of God made flesh, Jesus the Christ, has completed his 'mission' in the Cross and Resurrection, the love of God revealed there is only partially understood, for "the total exposition of this love in the world that is not divine and is opposed to God demanded that Jesus should take the path into the uttermost darkness, because otherwise there would always have been some matter that would not let itself be used for the exposition of God (Holy Spirit as Love, p.122). The disciples failed to grasp the meaning of Jesus' life: "…it is only the fulfillment of the mission of the Incarnation that can provide an overview and an interpretation of it. Only now has 'all the truth' in the Johannine sense been realised; only now is it ready to be interpreted" (TL, 3:73). The divine life is ever creative, ever new, always being new life. The Holy Spirit leads us to interpretation by means of inclusion.[1] The Spirit incorporates these when he indwells into the relationship of mutual love of the Father and the Son giving them a participation in it. We are led to an inner participation in the attitude of divine selflessness, which was given expression in the life of the Word made flesh, Jesus the Christ (Jn 1:14) (GL, vol 7, 429). Just as the Son poured himself out in becoming man (see Phil 2:6-11) so are believers poured out by the Spirit of Christ given them.

The Unselfing Activity of the Holy Spirit:[2]

Jesus calls us to die to self and grow in his love. "Love one another as I have loved you" (Jn 13:34). Von Balthasar follows Augustine in describing sin as a drive towards privacy, a desire not to be exposed to the claim of others or the vicissitudes of time. This view has been expressed well by his theological colleague and lifelong friend, Adrienne Von Speyr:

> "The world of flesh is an ego-world, the world of limitation, of selfish choice, of drawing all things to oneself, of the satisfaction and kindling of desires that are only functions of self… it is therefore the world of everlasting constriction, of a confinement that narrows down into himself like a spiral movement."
>
> (Von Speyr: The Victory of Love, 25-26)

---

[1] Nicholas Healy, The Eschatology of Hans Urs Von Balthasar: Being as Communion (Oxford: Oxford University Press, 2005) p.139.

[2] Jeffrey A. Vogel, The Unselfing Activity of the Holy Spirit in the Theology of Hans Urs Von Balthasar, Logos, vol 10, no.4, Fall 2007 - at questia.com

Similarly Gabriel Marcel understands sin, at root, as the act of shutting oneself in on oneself or taking one's own self as the centre.[3] As people called to union with God, human beings are estranged form their true nature by this self-enclosure.

In The Light of Christ Balthasar writes:

> "The ability to be poor is the human being's deepest wealth; this is revealed by the Christ event, in which the essence of being became visible for the very first time; as glory. In giving up his Son, God the Father has opened up this possibility for all. But the Spirit of God is sent to change this possibility into a reality. He shows the world the poverty of the Son, who sought only the glory of the Father and let himself be robbed of everything in utter obedience, was the most exact expression of the absolute fullness, which does not consist of being, but of "being = giving". It is in giving that one is and has."
>
> (GL, vol 7, p.391).

In the Old Testament God promised that he would write his law of love on human hearts, so that they would know God from within (Jer 31:33f; 2 Cor 3:3). The law of love is the Spirit: he himself (GL7;400).

The beloved is offered in love "in the act of the one who loves him, who offers him as he is in himself, and at the same time, as the one who is constituted this person through this act." (GL7:400). God promised us the highest gift of all – himself and life with him. He became flesh and was beloved "and indeed a beloved just as man is, turned away from love and deprived of glory" (GL7:401). We can take Paul's words seriously if God "did not spare his own son, but gave him up for us all, how could he not give us all things together with him" (Rom 8:32). In the Son God gives us himself totally. The kernel of faith means allowing

---

[3] Gabriel Marcel, The Mystery of Being, vol 11: Faith and Reality (South Bend, IN: Regency/Gateway, Inc:1951) p.181

God to love us, accepting that love and allowing him to lead us where he will. In making this act of self-surrender I am seized by love. The Spirit is the one who leads us into being children of God: "God sent the Spirit of his Son into our hearts, which cries out: 'Abba, beloved Father!'" (Gal 4:6). The Spirit is the pneuma of the Father also because it is only through him that we can be children (with the Son) drawn into the event of the eternal generation of the Son (Jn 1:13). We arrive precisely at the place that was destined for us before 'the foundation of the world'. (Eph 1:4f). We are no longer alienated from our true selves. We enter into the absolute love that we find ourselves (GL,7:405).

The Son snatches us from the slavery of sin, of the lack of love and selfishness, in order to bring us back to our true selves and God. The Spirit enables us to share in the prayer of Jesus who prays to the Father in the certainty that he is heard (Jn 11:42). We are told by Jesus to pray in the same manner in his name and in our state of abiding in him (Jn 14:13f; 15:7). "This is the confidence (Parrhesia)[4] that we have towards him: that he hears us when we pray in accordance with his will: and we know he hears us in whatever we ask, then we know too that we have already received what we ask from him." (1 Jn 5:14f).

Von Balthasar stresses the complete naturalness of this selflessness. Again he bases this view on the revelation of Jesus Christ:

> "Christ does not alienate man from himself when he raises
> him from the apparently closed substantiality of his
> personal being (in which he stands over against God) into
> an open relatedness of life with the Godhead. Rather Christ
> brings him into the genuine truth of his origin."
>
> (GL7:408f)

This leads us to see "None of us live for himself, and none of us die for himself; if we live we live to the Lord and if we die, we die to the Lord" (Rom 14:7f) and when we are loved we can hear Paul's injunction:

---

[4] Schlier, TDNT,V, 871-886.

"Bear one another's burdens, and then you will fulfill the law of Christ." (Gal 6:1). We learn to see the brother or sister for whom Christ died (see 1 Cor 8:11).

St. Francis was one such person who became unselfed. In losing his life he found it (see Mtt 16:25; Lk 17:33 etc.). He became one with the crucified. This was seen outwardly in his bearing of the wounds of the crucified. He was filled with the Spirit of Love and embraced all in compassion and love.

Enter the Darkness:

Faith's effect of 'unselfing' creates a vacant space that is occupied by Christ and his "Spirit" who confirms to us that we, like the son, are children of the Father (TD V, 334). The words are beautiful but in many of us who bear that wound that will not go away the words somehow seem distant. This brings me on to the crux of my work, how to remain faithful when other voices displace the positive ones. When it comes to the feeling of abandonment we find the figure of one who is more forsaken than ourselves.

In Dostoyevsky's novel "The Idiot" Myshkin finds himself beside his "brother" Rogozhin, the murderer of Natasha Philipovna. "The prince reached out his trembling hand and gently touched his head, his hair, stroking them and his cheeks ... there was nothing more he could do! ... at length he lay down on the cushions, as though in inner exhaustion or despair, and pressed his face against the motionless face of Rogozhin."[5] The inner exhaustion catches the essence of my pain – as it does for so many. It is from there we have to remain faithful. "The poor man" says Paul Claudel in one of his poems "has no friend to rely on except the one poorer than himself," and in the last line: "A poor man has at last found someone poorer: thus in silence, they look at one another."[6]

---

[5] The Idiot, trans. A. Myers (Collins:1992), 648.

[6] P. Claudel, Mother of Perpetual Help, conclusion of part 1 of the Corona poems.

St. John of the Cross (1542-1591): A Roadmap

John of the Cross was a Carmelite friar who was born at Fontiveros, old Castile. He was ordained priest in 1567 and thought of joining the strict Carthusian order. He met Teresa of Jesus in Medina and she convinced him to help her in her reforms of the Carmelite order. However there were tremendous tensions between the Carmelites doing the reform. One night in December 1577, a group of Carmelites opposed to reform broke into John's dwelling in Avila and took him prisoner. He spent eight months in prison in Toledo before he escaped.

John composed a series of works, no doubt informed by his experiences.[7] John comments: "The pains of hell encompassed me." Most vividly does the soul feel the deathly shadows, deathly sighs and the torments of hell. For it feels itself godless, punished and rejected by God, the object of his displeasure and wrath. The soul feels all this and more: it feels that this state will last for all eternity (Dark Night, II,8). Angela of Foligno speaks of a "terrifying darkness on God's part, from which hope is absent". I find Hell in myself. "Sometimes this experience is so vivid that it seems to the soul that it sees Hell and perdition before it. These are the ones who go down into Hell alive." (Living Flame of Love, 3:22). The soul feels terrible annihilation as an event in its very substance (Night, ii, 6:6), her hope in God vanishes and with it any prospect for an end to the night (Night, ii, 7:2-3). She resembles one who is imprisoned in a dark dungeon, bound hands and feet, and able neither to move, nor see, nor feel any favour from heaven or earth (Night ii, 7:3). A person is brought to think that they are far from any hope of blessing: the soul is convinced that all blessings have come to an end. Prayer becomes impossible for the soul: "it cannot be that God hears" (Night ii, 8:1). Yet in spite of appearances the soul is held in God's love.

This love penetrates and purifies the soul. It's effect is like the fire on wood. First the fire blackens and dries the wood, causes it to sweat and

---

[7] The Collected Works of St. John of the Cross, trans. Kieran Kavanagh, O.C.D. and Otilio Rodriguez, O.C.D. (Washington D.C.: Institute of Carmelite Studies, 1979). Vida y Obras de San Juan de la Cruz (Madrid: Biblioteca de Autores Cristianos, 1950).

thus envelopes it with smoke, but then when it has been purified in this way, the wood is burnt through from within and transformed into fire (Night ii, 10, 1-4). The soul finds peace. The divine sunlight flares up. There is an eruption of the habit of love in the act of love (Living Flame, i;3).

"For I know well the Spring that flows and runs
Although it is night."

He always looked to the figure of Christ. There is much to fathom in Christ, for he is like an abundant mine with unaccounted recesses of treasures, so that however deep men go they never reach the end or bottom, but rather in each recess they find new veins with new riches everywhere. (Canticle 36;3).

The soul feels the touches (toques) of God's love. John speaks of being branded with a branding iron, a wound of love, that unlike a bodily wound can be healed only by being deepened "until the soul at last is one single wound of love .... and so is healed by love" (Flame, II, 7). This is seen in St. Francis being branded with the wounds of the stigmata. St. John says: "You granted it to me through the caresses with which you caressed me, that is, through the effulgence of your glory and the image of your essence, your only Son. With him merciful hand of the Father, You have wounded me and deeply branded me" (Flame II, 7). The touches of love so inflame the soul that it is simultaneously "within their fire", seeming to be aflame with the Holy Spirit and yet on the other hand, it is the shadow cast by the divine light: "The shadow created on the soul by the torch of God's beauty is itself beauty, corresponding to the primal, divine beauty." (Flame III, 14). For John if the soul allows himself to be the recipient, it can retain all it receives just as it received it.

"...knowing, which prior to this union grasped things in a natural manner, by the power of its natural light and nourished by its senses, is henceforth in motion and is steered by something higher, by the primal power of the divine and supernatural light. Now, elevated above the

18

senses, it has become divine…, and its will, which loved heretofore in a base and mortal way with its natural feelings, is now transformed into the life of divine love, animated by the mighty breath of the Holy Spirit, in whom it already lives the life of love…. As a true daughter of God, the soul will move at the prompting of God's Spirit in all things. This is also Paul's teaching: All who are led by the Spirit of God are sons of God (Rom 8:14)…. Of course, the substance of the soul is not God's substance, and it cannot change itself into him; but since it is enveloped in God, it is God by participation in him."

(Flame, II, 14).

With all its being the soul strives to answer the love it receives. This becomes possible by the indwelling of the Spirit. "It can only attain this likeness by a total transformation of its will to the will of God…. this does not destroy the soul's will: it becomes God's will. Thus it loves God with the will of God, which is its own will: now it loves as much as it is loved, for it loves with the divine will, that is, through the Holy Spirit." (Canticle, stanza 37). So the breathing of the Holy Spirit by the Father and the Son also becomes a breathing on the part of the soul.

The Spirit forms and equips the soul so that, in God, it can carry out the same breathing of love that the Father fulfills in the Son and the Son in the Father. This breathing of love is the same Holy Spirit whom they breathe forth to one another in this transformation. For the transformation would not be genuine if the soul were not unveiledly and patently refashioned into the three Persons of the Most Holy Trinity…. The soul breathes God in God, and this breathing is the breathing of God himself…. It must not be thought impossible for the soul to desire something so sublime, for if God gives it grace to become God-like and united to the Most Holy Trinity, and so become God by participation, why should we not believe that it attains its insight, its knowledge and its love within the Trinity and in

participation in the Trinity, just as the latter does itself...
[albeit through] participation, since God is at work in it?

(Canticle; stanza 39, 3-6).

Jesus merited for us to become children of God (Jn 1:12-13) then Jesus prays to the Father asking him to send us where he is (Jn 17:24). Jesus prays that we be one as he and the Father are one (Jn 17:20-23). We become "partakers of the divine nature" (2 Peter 1:2-4). God involves us in his work of the new creation.

Chapter 2

Traumatic Intrusions

Yet there is often a day in the life that breaks up our minds. The well-ordered pattern of the previous chapter is destroyed forever. There is the infinite pain of a trauma that does not go away. The traumatic pain doesn't go away but resurfaces as nightmares, depression and post-traumatic stress. One feels terror, loss of control and utter helplessness. My own experience of abuse and bullying brought me to that place. All through my life this abuse was made real again and again. What is trauma? Trauma is an experience of being negatively overwhelmed, both physically and psychologically. Severe trauma destroys one's sense of self-protection, personal invulnerability and safety in a world that has lost all predictability. In many cases distraction pushes people to take their lives.

Bessel van der Kolk, a leading trauma therapist, notes that the inability to integrate the traumatic event into one's understanding of reality results in "repetitive replaying of the trauma in images, behaviours, feelings, physiological states and interpersonal relationships" (Traumatic Stress, p.43). Van der Kolk also says: "When the meaning of trauma is secret, forbidden, or unacceptable... trauma is unlikely to result in the mobilisation of external resources, in restitution or in the meting out of justice. Because of the lack of validation and support, traumatic events are more likely to play on the victims' minds." (Black Hole of Trauma, p.25).

Affliction and the Christian:

Simone Weil was a French philosopher (1909-1943). She will be with us on our journey. She felt a unique compassion for suffering humanity and longed to ease the pain of a lonely world. During the 1930s she worked as a laborer in a factory and she had the sensation of being crushed in mind and body. She described this situation as being one of affliction. She says this involves "social degradation or the fear of it in some form". Weil characterises a person who is afflicted as "a being struggling like a half-crushed worm", rendered incapable of even expressing the sense of mutilation he or she is experiencing (Waiting for God, p.120). She characterises affliction as stamping one's should like a red-hot iron with self-hatred, defilement and guilt that causes one to act self-destructively (Waiting for God, 122f). Wendy Farley argues that often victims of radical suffering are unable to defy evil and that they also participate in their own self-destruction. She says:

> "The sign of radical suffering is that the person is made inhuman by suffering. But the complicity of the self in its own destruction does not parallel the culpability of sin. The absence of even the desire for freedom from pain makes plain the hideous damage that suffering can do to the human spirit. Persons who are so badly hurt that they become accomplices in their own destruction, far from sharing responsibility for their defeat, are persons already broken by pain. Part of the terrible guilt borne by the victimiser lies in cruelty's power not only to hurt people but literally to destroy them."
> (Tragic Vision and Divine Compassion, p.58).

In this state of affliction one feels unworthy and in no way lovable. I know that place - as new traumas intrude I am brought back to that place again and again.

One attempt to deal with trauma involves "dissociating". This is an attempt to split off the traumatic events from consciousness. Dissociation refers to the capacity to separate the elements of the traumatic experience – emotions, thoughts, sensation, location, time and meaning – into shattered fragments that defy conscious integration. Another way is to blame oneself. A child who has been abused can blame himself or herself. It creates the illusion of a sense of control over the abuse and the hope that the abuse will end if the child is good (God and the Victim, p.42). These defence mechanisms do not work and the pain intrudes once more.

Anxiety is present as an almost constant companion. When stress comes, those abused can feel intensely and chronically confused, agitated, empty, isolated, anxious. One can feel panicked, furious, and in deep despair. Loneliness in more than just a word. It can lead to self-destructive behavior and aggression either against oneself or others.

The effect of abuse can destroy one's image of oneself. Judith Herman describes how one's self-image is fragmented in the following way:

> "All the structures of the self – the image of the body, the internalised image of others and the values and ideals that lend a sense of coherence and purpose – are invaded and systematically broken down… the victim of a single acute trauma may say she is "not herself" since the event, …the victim of chronic trauma may lose the sense that she has a self."
>
> (Complex PTSD, p.94f)

Some people struggle with alexithymia - feeling dead and lacking empathy for others. Those who have been abused feel that they cannot love any more. (Herman, Trauma and Recovery, p.111).

Tasso and Freud:

Torquato Tasso (1544-1595) was an Italian poet of the 16th century. He is best known for his poem "La Gerusalemme Liberata" (Jerusalem Delivered, 1581). He suffered from mental illness.

Tasso's poem contains the story of Tancred and Clorinda. Tancred slays his lover Clorinda in battle. She had disguised herself. Her soul is imprisoned in a tree. Tancred slashes at the tree with his sword and he hears Clorinda's voice cry out again and again from the tree. He kills her a second time. When Freud (1865-1939) wrote "Beyond the Pleasure Principle" (1920) he quoted this scene from Tasso. Up until World War I and its aftermath Freud believed in the 'pleasure principle' as a major driving force but in his work with those who were traumatised by war he noticed how the trauma came back to haunt the survivors in different ways.

He likened the fate of the war veterans to that of the tragic lovers - Tancred and Clorinda. The past is vividly enacted in the present in the form of flashbacks. The traumatic structure of the war experience is a literal enactment of a past that was not fully grasped at the point when it occurred. The original death event – the first slaying of Clorinda – is the unbearable content of comfort. As Tancred's experience suggests the unwitting return reveals the puzzling enigma of trauma. The trauma in the way it was not known in the first instance returns to haunt the survivor later on. (Caruth, Unclaimed Experience, p.21).

Trauma theory has evolved since Freud, but his use of Tasso highlights for us the unexpected ways trauma comes back and one feels overwhelmed, full of self-hatred and loneliness. To be with someone in this state and remain in silent compassion is often the only positive response. Counselling can bring one so far but in the end telling and re-telling one's story can lead to re-traumatisation.

Simone Weil:

I know that feeling of trauma – 'affliction' in Simone Weil's words. I also know that there are many aspects of the trauma I cannot verbalise. An inchoate foggy loneliness overwhelms me for a time. Yet in this experience unexpected shafts of light enter in. Simone Weil's story has often helped me. It does not take the pain away but I do perceive a little light breaking through. Her life was marked by an exceptional compassion for the suffering of others. When she was only six years old she refused to eat sugar because she heard that the soldiers at the front had no sugar. After her graduation in philosophy she became a teacher. She joined the Spanish Civil War on the side of the Anarchists and she worked in various auto-factories. This is when she spoke of affliction!

She had been reared as an agnostic. Weil visited Portugal and witnessed a religious procession. She could see in those on the procession her own image, they were the ones who knew 'affliction'. She was in Assisi in the Spring of 1937. She had a religious experience in the church of Santa Maria degli Angeli - the same church in which Francis of Assisi had prayed. Here in the tiny chapel Simone felt compelled to kneel down and pray.

She later attended the Benedictine Abbey of Solesmes in Belgium. Here she felt the attraction of God's love. She read George Hebert's poem Love.

"Love bade me welcome; yet my soul drew back,
Guilty of dust and sin.
But quick-eyed Love, observing me grow slack
From my first entrance in,
Drew nearer to me, sweetly questioning
If I lacked anything.
'A guest,' I answered 'worthy to be here':
Love said, 'You shall be he.'"

Simone said: 'Christ himself came down and took possession of me.' It is in affliction that she came to meet Jesus and her life afterwards was a communion with Jesus the Christ. It is in 'affliction' that we come to know in a new way Jesus the Christ. Even in the hell of trauma and 'affliction' we find that there is one who is there with us.

Spiritual Friends

Simone Weil is one of the little lights that help dispel my darkness. The tired-weary loneliness of the night of affliction is ultimately not the end – like Jimmy in Quadrophenia there is a light. The darkness is still there but love, the Holy Spirit, does intrude on the intrusion of trauma. Meditating on Holy Saturday with Hans Urs Von Balthasar and Adrienne Von Speyr helps me meet the wounded and lonely Jesus.

Hans Urs Von Balthasar (1905-1988) was a Swiss theologian and priest. Pope St. John Paul asked him as a favour to become a cardinal, but he died before the honour could be conferred. He was born in Lucerne in Switzerland. In 1923 he studied at the University of Zurich. He studied philosophy and German literature subsequently in Vienna and Berlin and culminated in his doctoral work on German literature and idealism. He joined the Jesuits and was ordained in 1936. He worked for a brief time on the Jesuit journal, Stimmen und Zeit. In 1940 with the Nazi regime encroaching on the freedom of Catholic journalists, he left Germany and worked in Basel as a student chaplain. While he was in Basel he met Adrienne Von Speyr.

Von Speyr was born in La Choux-de-Fonds, Switzerland. Adrienne was often ill but despite her suffering she helped others. In November 1917 she experienced a mystical vision of Our Lady. This led to a Marian character in her works. After her father's death Adrienne suffered a total physical collapse. The doctors thought she would die. She was sent to Leysin, where she was cared for by Charlotte Olivier, a relative by marriage and a doctor. There Adrienne would pray in a Catholic church. She felt she was being called to become a Catholic. Adrienne recovered and became a doctor.

In the summer of 1927 she met a history professor Emil Dürr, who had two sons. They married but he died suddenly in 1934. This led to a deep depression but Adrienne promised to live for God alone. This event was traumatic for Adrienne. She passed her state boards shortly after her wedding. She was the first woman in Switzerland to be admitted to the medical profession. In 1936 she married again. She married Werner Kaegi, an associate professor under Dürr. In 1940 she suffered a heart attack. She had expressed a wish to meet the new chaplain in Basel, Von Balthasar. They met in 1940 and later Von Balthasar received her into the church. She became a Catholic. She began to have mystical experiences. She entered into a mystical communion with Jesus in his suffering and death. Of special interest to us is her experience of Holy Saturday.

Von Balthasar released prayer in the heart of Von Speyr. While her husband Emil was dying she struggled with the words "Thy will be done". If it was God's will to take her husband then she could not pray for that (Von Balthasar, First Glance at Adrienne Von Speyr, p.31). The sorrow of losing her husband stayed with her when she married Werner Kaegi and she had a profound inability to pray the Our Father.

After the two met after Von Speyr's heart-attack, they walked together by the shore of the Rhine. They spoke about the Catholic poets, Paul Claudel and Charles Péguy. It was then Von Speyr asked to become a Catholic. They started to talk about her prayer and her inability to pray the Our Father. Von Balthasar told her that the prayer means "we offer him our willingness to let what he does take over our lives and move us anywhere at will" (First Glance, 57f). He also taught her the simply repetitive, unself-conscious way of praying the Our Father. Immediately she recovered her prayer-life and was carried away by a flood of prayer as if a dam had burst (First Glance, p.31). After this she received baptism. She understood her baptism as a dying and rising that only God could accomplish. On the day of her baptism she wrote in her diary: "Pour aujourd'hui il n'y a qu'un mot, un seul: merci [For me there is nothing but one word, one alone: thank you] (First Glance, p.119).

Holy Saturday:

Von Balthasar tells us:

> "Every year the passion ended on Good Friday, at about three o'clock in the afternoon, with a death-like trance into which flashed the thrust of the lance. Then shortly afterwards began "the descent into hell" (which lasted into the early morning hours of Easter Sunday) about which Adrienne gave detailed accounts year after year."
>
> (First Glance, p.65).

This is Von Balthasar's description of Adrienne's experience of the "descent into hell". In 1941 and for the next twenty-five years, Speyr gave an account of her experience of the descent. On Holy Saturday she experienced a suffering that went beyond death. She said: "I didn't feel anything physically on Holy Saturday... I felt only a great weariness.. a soul-condition." (Speyr, Kreuz und Hölle, I, vol 3, p.36). She describes the suffering as more psychological than physical, the anguish stemming from what was absent rather than that that was present. There was extreme loneliness, forsakenness and abandonment in this pain. The pain of hell meant she was cut off from all relationships. Just as the Son is cut off from the love of the Father, Speyr entered into this brokenness. In reading Von Speyr's description of this state I am led once again to the pain of trauma. Von Speyr entered this pain and experienced the loneliness and abandonment of this pain. She became Von Balthasar's theological partner and her experiences helped inform his work. Von Balthasar interpreted her share in Christ's suffering as a gift. He said "Perhaps our time is ripe for the blessing" (Einleitung, in Kreuz und Hölle, vol 3, 10). He referred here particularly to her Easter Saturday experience.

Von Balthasar wrote "Das Herz der Welt" [Heart of the World] in 1943. In it he gives his first attempt at reflection on Von Speyr's experience. The incarnation is described using the image of the heart. The incarnation is the descent of God's heart into the world, and the events of Jesus's life, death and resurrection are all described as the process by which the divine heart seeks to transform the human heart. Holy Saturday is a pivotal part of the divine love story. It narrates divine love at its least discernible point – between death and resurrection, in the abyss of hell. Von Balthasar uses the Gospel of John in his reflection.

In chapter 9 in "The Heart of the World" Von Balthasar describes a witness at the foot of the cross. The chapter is entitled "A Wound has Blossomed". The witness attempts to articulate the post death events. The witness stands in the space of death, surrounded by a darkness thicker than she has ever known. Jesus appears defeated: "Suddenly all of them standing around the gallows know it: he is gone. Immeasurable emptiness (not solitude) streams forth from the hanging body. Nothing but the fantastic emptiness is any longer at work here." (Heart of the World, p.150).

Then something strange happens. What is it? She does not know. She believes she saw a tiny, moving light. "Is that death?... Is it the end?...

Is it the beginning? The beginning of what?" (Heart, p.152). She witnesses in these postcrucifixion moments something that survives death. The drama becomes a theo-drama, a drama in which the Father and Holy Spirit are involved.

Between passion and resurrection there is no light, no life and no words. It is that pain of anguish we feel when we cannot express our grief in trauma. Von Balthasar insists that Jesus did not descend into hell as risen but as dead (Saward, The Mysteries of March, p.113). He is dead with the dead in hell. Von Balthasar develops his insights in his works "Mysterium Paschale" and "Theo-Drama" (vols 4,5). On Holy Saturday the Son descends as dead into the abyss of hell. It is neither a stunning picture of victory. On the cross, the Son takes on the sins of the world. His mother takes all the sadness of the world to herself. The cross is a self-surrender of the Son. He is dead and the landscape of the hell he enters is a landscape of death and a vision of sin in its rawest form. For Von Balthasar the descent is the climax of the narrative of Jesus' passion:

> "The paschal mystery means that God, in love, has entered into the hiatus of death – physical and spiritual – and has taken the full measure of our situation not from the outside as it were, but from the inside, sharing our desolation, bearing our sin, as Son experiencing God-forsakenness."
> (Anne Hunt, The Trinity and the Paschal Mystery, p.80).

On this day Jesus experiences what it means to be far from the Father. Jesus' suffering means he is infinitely lonely. When I am in loneliness, I find myself praying and there the figure of the lonely one sustains me.

In Von Balthasar's collection of sermons "You Crown the Year with Your Goodness" (1982) he preaches about Easter but he refers explicitly to Holy Saturday. In Hell Jesus perceives something like a bridge leading him out of Hell (You Crown, p.91). It is something like a bridge; it is lightly built; it is a connective thread. Balthasar's language is paradoxical. The Holy Spirit is the one who bridges the rift, but he is not the bridge. We can imagine that grace, faith and prayers weave around this thread, strengthening it to hold the weight of those crossing. The Spirit inspires the prayers of the faithful to aid the vulnerable Jesus. He gives certain souls a special share in this suffering. They console the lonely Jesus - in himself and in his brothers and sisters.

In our journey from Hell the passage is not smooth. We have to trust in Jesus. We are supported by the Holy Spirit when we do not know how to pray properly (Rom 8:26). The Father is the one who guides the process. He holds all people in the palm of his hand.

In the aftermath of death, Balthasar says we are like "disoriented, half-dead flies" (p.87). The rescue from the abyss is not being spared from the death. In the death and loss of self that abuse produces, there is a death and loss of self. The descent into Hell and the resurrection help us see that the pain is not final or ultimate. Death is pulled into life and the little light that flickers becomes the new light of life. Our journey through trauma and pain is a journey with the dead Christ to new life. We bear the wounds of the crucified.

Chapter 3

Worse than Death

Von Balthasar wrote an article in Communio[1] in 1981 called "Plus Loin que la mort." In it he gives a brief introduction to his work on Holy Saturday. In it he reminds us to take seriously Jesus' death and descent into Hell. In it he points out that this death goes further than any other death. Jesus encounters those who have died and feels their estrangement. Yet thanks to the figure of Saint Thérèse of Lisieux therein lies our hope. We dare hope that thanks to Jesus' experience of hell (Sheól, hadès, infernum) his mercy reaches out to even those who appear most lost. He ends the article with a quote from the Canticle of Canticles, "Love is as strong as death" (Canticle 8:6) – no, says Von Balthasar, it is even stronger.

Von Balthasar's "Heart of the World" foreshadows the works of his maturity. Andrew Louth points out that this work is an uncanny crystallization of the vision of Adrienne Von Speyr as indeed Von Balthasar later sketched it in his introductory work to Adrienne's writings, "First Glance at Adrienne Von Speyr".[2] For Von Balthasar, Speyr's experience of Holy Saturday must be located within the testimonies of charismatic experiences of the company of Christian mystics and saints throughout the history of the church and sheds light on the experience of Jesus experience. This does not prompt him to leave Scripture behind. Rather it informs his reading of Scripture. Jesus died for us (the "pro-nobis" of the creed). Balthasar sought an understanding of this mystery and through his works inspires us with an insight into this mystery.

---

[1] see Von Balthasar, Plus loin que la mort, Communio, no. VI, 1 - Janvier Février, 1981, p.2-5.

[2] see Andrew Louth, "The Place of the Heart of the World in the Theology of Hans Urs Von Balthasar, in The Analogy of Beauty, ed. John Riches (Edinburgh, T. & T. Clark, 1986)

Adrienne Von Speyr's Gift and 'Heart of the World'

The fundamental structure of Adrienne's vision is Marian. At its heart is Mary's yes to God. It is in this light we understand her emphasis on obedience. 'Heart of the World', as we saw, was written out of the initial impact of his friendship with Von Speyr. Von Balthasar said that the effect of Adrienne coming to Catholicism was the unleashing of an apprehension of the dimensions of a faith that previously had been pent up (First Glance, p.31). He had the sense of barriers broken down and a stream of experiences and insights came flooding out. Von Balthasar describes Speyr's experience as follows:

> "From 1941 on, year after year – in the interior experiences which she has described – she was allowed to share in the suffering of Christ... A landscape of pain of undreamt-of variety was disclosed to me, who was permitted to assist her: how many and diverse were the kinds of fear, at the Mount of Olives and at the Cross, how many kinds of shame, outrage and humiliation, how many forms of Godforsakenness, of Christ's relation to the sin of the world, quite apart from the inexhaustible abundance of physical pain. Christ's passion, viewed from within, is of a diversity which the biblical texts and images leave hidden; but numerous mystics throughout the centuries have been allowed to experience a great deal of it in ever-varying aspects - if only by drops, as it were, compared with the Son of God."
>
> (First Glance, p.64f)

Balthasar provides us with an interpretation of the theological significance of Speyr's own descent into Hell which began annually on Good Friday afternoon and lasted until Easter Sunday morning. This interpretation highlights Jesus' acceptance and points out the saving effect (the "pro-nobis") which will be the focus of much of Balthasar's later work.

"It is Christ's final act of obedience towards his Father that he descends 'into hell' (or 'underworld', Hades, Sheol). Because hell is (already in the Old Covenant) the place where God is absent, where there is no longer the light of faith, hope, love, of participation in God's life; hell is what the judging God condemned and cast out of his creation; it is filled with all that is irreconcilable with God, from which he turns away for all eternity. It is filled with the reality of all the world's godlessness, with the sum of the world's sin; therefore, with precisely all of that from which the Crucified has freed the world. In hell he encounters his own work of salvation, not in Easter triumph, but in the uttermost night of obedience, truly the 'obedience of a corpse.' He encounters the horror of sin separated from men. He 'walks' through sin (without leaving a trace, since, in hell and in death, there is neither time nor direction); and, traversing its formlessness, he experiences the second chaos. While bereft of any spiritual light emanating from the Father, in sheer obedience, he must seek the Father where he cannot find him under any circumstances. And yet, this hell is a final mystery of the Father as the creator (who made allowances for the freedom of man). And so, in this darkness, the Incarnate Son learns 'experientially' what until then was 'reserved' for the Father. Hell, seen in this way, is, in its final possibility, a Trinitarian event.

(First Glance, p.65)

In "Heart of the World" he describes Jesus as he faces the prospect of bearing the weight of humanity's sin, its violence, rejection and hate and enduring the pain of separation that the sin involves – the complete separation and isolation from God his Father. Balthasar uses the words of enduring God's judgement of this sin through abandonment and forsakenness. Balthasar's association with Karl Barth, a famous Protestant theologian in Basel at the same time, influenced his idea of 'substitutionary' atonement. Jesus took our place. He describes Jesus' experience as follows:

What you suffer is a shapeless fear. It is a sea without shores, fear-in-itself. The fear which is the core of sin. The fear of God and his inescapable judgement. The fear of hell. The fear of never again seeing the face of the Father for all eternity. The fear that love itself and every creature with it have dropped you irretrievably into the abyss. You fall into the bottomless; you are lost. Not the faintest shimmer of hope delimits this fear.

(Heart of the World, p.109)

Balthasar uses poetic language to show us Jesus' suffering. The extent to which the love of God will go to redeem and heal broken and fallen humanity is seen in the depths to which Jesus Christ descends in his experience of abandonment in the loneliness of hell. His death involves the terror of abandonment, the feeling of utter loneliness, isolation and non-existence. The death of Jesus reached beyond mere physical suffering and transported him in his very soul to the depths of hell, to the extremity of separation from God and from life. "Immeasurable emptiness (not solitude) streams forth from the hanging body. Nothing but this fantastic emptiness..." (Heart, p. 150). It is Good Friday. Then we follow Jesus in his descent into Hell. We enter the chaos of Holy Saturday. There we find: "Chaos. Beyond heaven and hell. Shapeless nothingness behind the bounds of creation. Is that God? God died on the Cross. Is that death? No dead are to be seen. Is it the end? Nothing that ends is any longer there." (Heart, p.150). Then all is: "Quiet, quiet... it's still too early in the day to think of hope." (Heart, p.151). Yet there is already the faint hope of a new beginning - the Holy Spirit hovers over this desolation.

"It is a beginning without parallel, as if Life were arising from Death, as if weariness (already such weariness as no amount of sleep could ever dispel) and the uttermost decay of power were melting at creation's outer edge, were beginning to flow, because flowing is perhaps a sign and a likeness of weariness which can no longer contain itself, because everything that is strong and solid must in the end dissolve into water. But hadn't it – in the beginning – also been born from water? And is this wellspring in the chaos, this trickling weariness, not the beginning of a new creation?"

(Heart, p.152)

The 'Heart of the World' is the Sacred Heart, the Heart of love in Jesus:

"The divine Ocean forced into the tiny wellspring of a human Heart! The mighty oak-tree of divinity planted in the small, fragile pot of an earthly Heart! God, sublime on the throne of his majesty, and the Servant - toiling with sweat and kneeling in the dust of adoration - no longer to be distinguished from one another! The eternal God's awareness of his kingship pressed into the nescience of human abasement! All the treasures of God's wisdom and knowledge stored in the narrow chamber of human poverty! The vision of the eternal Father shrouded in the intuitions of faith's obscurity! The rock of divine certainty floating on the tides of an earthly hope! The triangle of the Trinity balanced by one tip upon a human Heart!"

(Heart, p.49)

The Trinity is revealed in the Heart of the Son. The Heart of love descends into the extreme Hell of loneliness, of feeling nothingness – so that God's mercy can reach the one who feels utter abandonment and loneliness. Jesus is there before us. The true miracle of Jesus' Heart is revealed in the love that helped him say 'yes' to the Father's will.

"...that the perfect Yes to the Father's will could be uttered in the midst of a storm of impulses impelling the death-tormented Lamb to take flight; that the eternal distance of love between Father and Son (eternally enfolding the one in the other by the embrace of both in the Spirit) could become the yawning gap between heaven and hell, from whose pit the Son groans his 'I thirst', the Spirit now no longer anything but the huge, separating and impassable chaos; that the Trinity could, in suffering's distorted image, so disfigure itself into the relationship between judge and sinner..."

(Heart, p.54)

Jesus' apparent utter failure and weakness in the end bear fruit, and new life does come to be in the mystery of Easter Sunday and Pentecost.

Yet there is the weak breaking through of light. It is not the Holy Spirit but the light does ultimately come from him. The mother of Jesus, Mary and the Beloved Disciple began their vigil of prayer at the foot of the Cross (Jn 19:21-25) and their silent prayer continues. This is inspired and in the Holy Spirit. It is this that allows the light to come into the abyss and ultimately leads to Easter Day, when Jesus rises from the dead.

My experience of abuse is one that comes back. The trauma never quite goes away. When I had cancer the dark feelings came back again as if for the first time. Yet I felt sustained somehow. A friend of mine that I had not seen for years was led by the Spirit to pray for me because she knew I was ill - remember there was no earthly contact between us. Yet her prayer and the support of family and friends gave me strength when I felt I had none. The deep pain I was in became somehow bearable and the result of the operation was miraculous. I realised that my mental pain and its recurrence was my Holy Saturday experience. The lonely Christ was one with me and some people were led to be with me in prayer and share my desolation.

"Look, this is my secret, and there is no other in heaven or on earth: My Cross is salvation, my Death is victory, my Darkness is light. At that time, when I hung in torment and dread rushed into my soul because of the forsakenness, rejectedness, and uselessness of my suffering, and all was gloomy, and only the seething rage of that mass of teeth hissed up mockingly at me, while heaven kept silence, shut tight as the mouth of a scoffer (but through the open gates of my hands and feet my blood bubbled out in spurts, and with each throb my Heart became more desolate, strength poured out from me in streams and there remained only

36

faintness, death's fatigue, infinite failure), and at last I neared that mysterious and final spot on the very edge of being, and then - the fall into the void, the capsizing into the bottomless abyss, the vertigo, the finale, the un-becoming: that colossal death which only I have died. Through my death this has been spared you, and no one will ever experience what it really means to die: This was my victory." (Heart, p.175)

Bought at a Great Price:

St. Paul tells us: "For you were bought with a price: therefore glorify God in your body" (1 Cor 6:20). Using this text Balthasar preached on the significance of Jesus' passion:

> "'Bought at a great price.' The first Christians were well aware of this when they put these two little words, 'pro nobis,' at the heart of the Creed. It was 'for us' that the Son came down from heaven, 'for us' that he was crucified, died and was buried. And this means not only 'for our benefit' but also 'in our place', taking over what was our due. If this is watered down, the fundamental tenet of the New Testament disappears and it looks as if God is always reconciled, sin is always forgiven and overcome, irrespective of Christ's self-surrender; then the Cross becomes merely a particularly eloquent symbol of God's unchanging kindness, only a symbol, indicating something but not effecting anything. There would no longer be a Lamb of God who takes away the sins of the world. No longer would God 'reconcile the world to himself', as Paul explicitly says, 'through his Son'. Without noticing it, we have become like the men of the Enlightenment, aware of God's kindly disposition but refusing to countenance his anger over sin, of which Scripture speaks so insistently, because it does not fit in with our enlightened concept of God; in the end we make it all into an anemic, transparent

philosophy. Then, as a result, what Grünewald endeavored to portray in his crucifixion seems to us to be a tasteless medieval exaggeration. And the high price becomes a cheap price; costly grace becomes cheap grace."

(You Crown the Year, p.78f)

The idea of cheap grace is something about which Bonhoeffer spoke. Jesus does something that is impossible for anyone else to do. By entering the passion Jesus overcomes the power of sin and death and opens up new life for us in God. He takes our place in experiencing Godforsakenness and isolation. The gravity of what Jesus did is seen in his asking to be spared the 'cup' of suffering (Mk 14:26). The cup is the experience of being in the place of sin and sinners. He accepts this place because it is God's will. Balthasar describes the horror and pain of the experience of loneliness and apparently abandoned by the Father.

"The man who cries out knows only that he is forsaken; in this darkness he no longer knows why. He is not permitted to know why, for the idea that the darkness he is undergoing might be on behalf of others would constitute a certain comfort; it would give him a ray of light. No such comfort can be granted him now, for the issue, in absolute seriousness, is that of purifying the relationship between God and the guilty world."

(Crown the Year, p.84)

This can only be accomplished because of Jesus' unique relationship to the Father. Jesus, by taking the effects of sin to himself, heals the division between God and fallen humanity. In the words of Balthasar he experiences God's 'wrath'.

"Jesus, the Crucified, endures our inner darkness and estrangement from God, and he does so in our place. It is all the more painful for him, the less he has merited it... it is utterly alien and full of horror. Indeed, he suffers more deeply than an ordinary man is capable of suffering, even were he condemned and rejected by God, because only the incarnate Son knows who the Father really is and what it means to be deprived of him, to have lost him (to all appearances) forever."

(Crown the Year, p.85)

It is the death of the eternal Son of God who 'was made flesh' (Jn 1:14). Balthasar points to other texts from St. Paul. These passages include: 2 Cor 5:14, 'one has died for all, therefore all have died'; 5:19, 'in Christ God was reconciling the world to himself'; 5:21, 'For our sake he made him to be sin, who knew no sin, so that in him we might become the righteousness of God'; and Gal 3:13, 'Christ redeemed us from the curse of the law, having become a curse for us'.

Paul Tillich spoke of this salvation in terms of acceptance. God loves us and accepts us. Faith is the courage to accept acceptance. We are loved unconditionally and without restriction. The Cross is "at the very heart of Christianity and makes possible the courage to affirm faith in the Christ; namely that in spite of all the forces of separation between God and man, this is overcome from the side of God." (The Dynamics of Faith, p.123). It is in accepting the pain of rejection and violence that this loving acceptance is seen. In the resurrection this love is stronger than death and is offered to us.

Tillich's words are not the same as Balthasar's. The mystery of Jesus' suffering is something both men tried to grapple with. No words are sufficient. Both viewpoints complement each other, but in the end God's actions cannot be contained in our words. He is always greater than our words.

Tillich said that spirit filled prayer has a healing effect on the human person (Eternal Now, p63,115) through the elevation to the centre of the personality to God (Systematic Theology 1:127). The word for 'save' and 'heal' in Greek is the same word, 'soter'. Prayer engenders in the human person the ability to accept the fact that one is accepted and loved by God in Jesus. In the depths of loneliness and deep anguish there is one who has been there before us in hell and the pain of isolation begins to crumble. The Son goes through Hell in order to return to the

Father. Yet he does not return alone. To all who accept love and mercy from him he brings them to the Father too. It is in this light that we understand the resurrection. "The Son must inspect whatever in the realm of creation is imperfect, deformed, chaotic so as to lead into his own possession as Redeemer..." (Mysterium Paschale, p.249)

The Attack of Darkness

Jesus' experience of abandonment is timeless. It is analogous to hell (TD, IV, p.337). This is why its actuality persists through all ages of the world. Jesus' agony lasts until the end of the world (Pascal). In fact it goes right back to the world's beginning. His mortal wounds are eternally open (Bérulle). This timelessness is confirmed in some precision by those Christian mystics who were privileged to experience something of the dark night of the Cross. "Where the should is seized by purifying contemplation, it feels in the most vivid manner death's shadow, its groanings and the pains of hell. For it feels God-less, punished and rejected by God, the object of his displeasure and anger. The soul feels all this and more: it seems to the soul that this condition will last forever." (John of the Cross, The Dark Night, II 6.2 to II 9). Each attack of darkness seems eternal.

The cup mentioned in the Mount of Olives is God's cup of wrath often referred to in the Old Covenant (e.g. Is 51:17; Jer 13:13, Ezek 23:32-34), Hab 2:15-16 etc.). It is filled with the wine of God's anger (Jer 25:16; Rev 14:8). It enters into the one who drinks it (Jer 25:16; Rev 14:8). Von Balthasar speaks about the cup of God's wrath (TD IV, p.338f) and it is easy to take too literally the language he uses. In the New Testament we see Jesus filled with "anger" and "grief" (Mk 3:5) at the Pharisees' hard-heartedness, which increases with every new sign of God's love, until they eventually lead him to die.

Jesus is angry with the rebellious enemies of God. He is deeply moved at the face of the power of death (Jn 11:33-38). He is appalled at the demonic in man (Jn 8:44) particularly the hypocrisy of the Pharisees (Mtt 15:7 passim), "this brood of vipers" (Mtt 12:34). We read that Jesus was in "warm indignation" (Mk 1:41-42 NEB) at a leper's condition. Jesus constantly upbraids the disciples who fail to recognize him: "How long am I to bear with you" (Mtt 17:17). Balthasar quotes the Jewish writer Abraham Heschel (TD IV p.343) and uses his idea of pathos to help us understand the terms God's anger, the cup of wrath.

Abraham Joshua Heschel (1907-1972) escaped from Europe a week before Hitler invaded Poland. He lost his family in the Holocaust. He'd dedicated his life to teaching, to recall people to their dignity made as they are in the image and likeness of God (Gen 1:16f). His major work was 'The Prophets'. The first pages of this book helped me understand so much of the prophets and ultimately Jesus. He tells us the sort of crimes that we take for granted cause the prophets heartache: Amos shows us the things the prophets care about:

"Hear this, you who trample upon the needy,
And bring the poor of the land to an end,
Saying: When will the new moon be over
That we may sell grain."

(Amos 8:4-6)

"To us a single act of injustice - cheating in business; exploitation of the poor is slight: to the prophets a disaster. To us injustice is injurious to the welfare of the people; to the prophets it is a deathblow to existence; to us, an episode; to them a catastrophe, a threat to the world."(Prophets, p.4). The rabbis said "Whoever destroys a single soul should be considered the same as one who has destroyed a whole world. And whoever saves a single soul is to be considered the same as one who has saved a whole world." (Prophets, p.14). The prophet is burdened with God's compassion for the world and his aim to conquer callousness and cruelty, to change the inner man. (Prophets, p.17). Heschel tells us that God does not stand outside the range of human suffering and sorrow. He is personally involved in, even stirred by, the conduct and fate of men (Prophets, p.224). God's participation in human history ...finds its deepest expression in the fact that God can actually suffer (Prophets, p.259). This care and concern God has in love, Heschel calls the pathos of God (Prophets p.223-224). This shows why God is angry – he hates injustice, cruelty, hardness, the suffering of the vulnerable and all that destroys us as humans. "The seed of Moloch is the death of man, the seed of the Lord is the life of man" (Man is Not Alone, p.245). Jesus came to reveal this face of God. God is love (1 Jn 4:9,16) and cares for his people. He is angry at lack of love and cruelty and all that keeps us from truly living. Yet he is left in loneliness. Jeremiah the prophet tried to call people to God's ways but he was rejected and left isolated.

> "Cursed be the day
> on which I was born...
> Because he did not kill me in the womb;
> So my mother would have been my grave.
>
> (Jeremiah 20:14-17)

Amos, too, found he was rejected:

> "They hate him who reproves in the gate,
> They abhor him who speaks the truth."
>
> (Amos 5:10)

People ultimately are afraid of the truth. We do not like the dark side, the shadow side of our personality to be revealed. We can becomes slaves to what others want of us so we can feel accepted. In chapter 10 of John's Gospel we read of the crowd piling up stone to kill Jesus. Jesus answers: "I have shown you many good works from the Father. For which of these are you going to stone me" (Jn 10:32). It is often not the unjust that we suspect but the good. Jesus' light is too bright for some and they kill him to quench that light. This is how we see Jesus fulfill the Father's will. He came to bring love but he was rejected and died. But God raised him on the third day, the day after Holy Saturday. This show us what lies behind the language used by Von Balthasar.

Resurrection, Spirit and Life in God

In the Gospel of Mark we find the women came to the tomb and they found the stone rolled back (Mk 16:4). Then they meet a young man who tells them that Jesus has been raised (Mk 16:6). They are confused by all these things and "... they went out and fled from the tomb, for terror and amazement had seized them; and they said nothing to anyone for they were afraid" (Mk 16:8). In the Gospel of John Mary Magdalene mistakes Jesus for the gardener (Jn 20:5). Coming to terms with this new event was disconcerting – yet all our reflections grow from the fact of Jesus being raised from the dead. The words of the Crucified feature in his resurrection and transfiguration (see Jn 20:26-30). His tortured body has been spiritualised – yet a hand can reach inside the wound in his body (Jn 20:27). He has passed to a state of eternal life beyond death (Rom 6:9). This is a drama experienced by the Trinity and is constantly actual (TD IV, p.363). All the more since the frame of the passion, to which the Eucharist belongs, embraces all past and future parts of world time. The one who died and experienced Hell now lives to God (Rom 6:10). He now stands at the right hand of God (Acts 7:55) and prays for God's people. He is given the keys of death and hell (Rev 1:18); because of his obedience unto death on the cross, he is given authority over heaven, earth and the nether world (Phil 2:9). He has conquered death and his mercy extends to all people. Now in freedom he sends forth the Spirit, who is his Spirit, the spirit of love, obedience and freedom (TD IV, p.364). 'Where the Spirit of the Lord is, there is freedom' (2 Cor 3:17). The entire movement of the Spirit is to lead us in the risen Christ's sonship. We are loved by the Father and we are precious to him. "See what love the Father has given us; that we should be called children of God and that is what we are". (1 Jn 3:1).

What we call evil, demonic, the devil, is the power that is hostile to God. God did not intend death as we experience it (see Wis 2:23-24). St. Paul tells us that Christ must reign "until he has put all his enemies under his feet. The last enemy to be destroyed is death" (1 Cor 15:26).

In his experience of hell Jesus experienced the ultimate loneliness. Those who are depressed and suffer from traumatic stress feel that this is the ultimate. Yet we find one who was more lonely than we are. His resurrection shows us that this infinite loneliness was not the end and in the power of the Spirit we are led to share his victory.

"The sphere in which the Christian lives which is summed up in the term 'in Christ' (*en Christoi*) embraces both the historical Christ and equally the risen Christ, who recapitulates in himself everything earthly", says Von Balthasar (TD IV, P.385). The idea of recapitulation is that Jesus takes everything to himself and transforms it – death is transformed into life. Our loneliness can be the place where we meet him and find we are loved. We can begin to let the light in and hope for healing. The term 'in Christ' used by Paul to show our incorporation into his life can also mean to be led by the Spirit. Resurrection in the full sense belongs to the life to come but even now we can begin to feel its effects.

Some souls are asked to work with Christ in his healing mission. We have seen Adrienne Von Speyr. Others that come to my mind are Clare of Assisi, Angela of Foligno, Thérèse of Lisieux and Mother Teresa. They live out what is said in the letter to the Colossians: "I complete what is lacking in the sufferings of Christ" (Col 1:24). The sufferings of the God-man are all-sufficient but he left room for others to work with him (see also Jn 16:1-4, Mtt 10:24f). Through grace a fellowship of suffering and resurrection is created. Jesus' teaching on the vine and branches shows us this (Jn 15:1-12). Those who suffer from trauma and feel that pain which comes back in the strangest ways and in different times have a special sharing in this fellowship. They share Jesus' loneliest hour and in sharing are on a journey to the resurrection. We find we are no longer alone. The worst thing about abuse and other traumatic experiences is that we feel we cannot talk or put words on the experience. However, when we find the lonely Jesus we can sit in silence – in a profound communion and there find love. From this experience we can be with others and in silent compassion with those who cannot talk let them know they are loved. In prayer too we can be silent with the lonely Jesus praying at all times for a lonely world.

Chapter 4

Martyrs as Witnesses

Some films such as The Truman Show (1998), The Matrix (1999) and American Beauty (1999) highlight the contrast between the happy, clean, middle class values that our culture commends and which, at some level, is what we end up striving for and the underlying reality of people who wear masks all the time, and who have a real struggle to come to grips with what is real and worthwhile in life. People who have suffered trauma and abuse find themselves wearing masks to blend in imagining that they are the only ones to feel pain.

Von Balthasar often spoke of how artists and writers were far ahead of the theologians and philosophers in expressing reality. I take his point and I extend it to the world in which one feels deep pain and an infinite sorrow, for instance I have always been haunted by the music of Supertramp. One of their songs "Rudy" is particularly poignant. It comes from the 1974 album "Crime of the Century":

> "Rudy's on a train to nowhere, halfway down the line
> He don't want to get there, but he needs time
> He ain't sophisticated, nor well educated
> After all the hours he wasted, still he needs time.
> He needs time - he needs time for livin',
> He needs time - for someone just to see him.
> He ain't had no lovin'
> For no reason or rhyme."

The image of a train to nowhere is a powerful one to show how lonely life can be. Rudy needs time, in other words hope that someone might see him. He might find he is valuable and precious as a person, but

> "All through for life, all through the years
> Nobody loved, nobody cared.
> So dim the light, dark are your fears

Try as I might, I can't hold back the tears
How can you live without love, it's not fair."

To be unloved is a hard burden. I know that feeling from times in hospital when for all intents and purposes I was abandoned. 'Nobody loved, nobody cared'. It is hard (maybe impossible) to live without love. We wear masks to hide ourselves and cry alone.

Yet there is light. In a later album "Even in the Quietest Moments" (1977), Roger Hodgson spoke of the song that gave the album its title. He says of the lyrics, "It's a kind of dual love song - it could be to a girl or it could be to God."[1]

"Even in the quietest moments
I wish I knew what I had to do
And even though the sun is shining
Well I feel the rain... here it comes again, dear
And even when you showed me
My heart was out of tune
For there's a shadow of doubt that's not letting me find you
too soon
The music that you gave me
The language of my soul
Oh Lord, I want to be with you.
Won't you let me come in from the cold?
Don't you let the sun fade away.
....."

It's like a cry from Rudy to feel a "heavenly caress" to comfort him and allow him "to come in from the cold". It catches the mood of waiting, waiting for someone, for God, for Godot to come and heal us. In their way Hodgson and Supertramp reflect to me the loneliness and insecurity of the pain that is sometimes too powerful.

[1] Martin Meluish, The Supertramp Book, (Toronto: Omnibus Press: 1986), p. 119.

Witnesses

When writers or artists pour out their pain in their work those who read or hear or look upon feel they are not alone. In some cases there can be the beginning of a healing because their pain is shared. The cross and Easter Saturday experience of Jesus should be understood in terms of a refusal to back down in the face of oppression and evil, and Jesus' willingness to stand for healing, mercy and justice for the least and the outcasts - even at the penalty of torture and death.[2] God's own self enters into human suffering via the incarnation, and the cross becomes a symbol of God's eternal solidarity with all who suffer. It is more than that because Jesus as the word of God made flesh takes to himself the full impact of sin and by his resurrection shows that love is stronger than death - is stronger than all the hatred, rejection and violence of a world that has grown hard and callous. His sending of the Spirit enables us to enter that new life. Easter Saturday and the pain of loss shows us Jesus take all of the creatures' pain and suffering into God's own being. Healing begins when our pain is recognised, when our cry is heard and our pain is God's pain and through this recognition and receiving, the transformation of our pain into new life. The mystery of Good Friday, Easter Saturday is a divine-human journey, through torture, death, the isolation of a lonely hell, gives new meaning to our terror and anguish. The resurrection becomes a sign of the new life that is possible beyond pain and suffering.[3] It is not only a redemption from sin, but from all grief of trauma and rejection.

To help those who suffer Stern uses the term witness to describe our role. "In relationship we are called into being by acts of recognition by the other".[4] He argues that the mind itself is brought into being by acts of recognition by primary caretakers. Balthasar in his personalist theology argues that we come to know love firstly by the love and smile

---

[2] See Bonnie J. Miller-McElmore; Suffering in The Blackwell Companion to Practical Theology, ed. B.J. Miller-McElmore (Oxford: Wiley 2012), p.28: Her article influenced greatly the next part of my work.

[3] J. Moltmann, Eschatology in R. Hunter and N. Ramsay; eds; Dictionary of Pastoral Care and Counselling, (Nashville: Abingdon Press, 2005), p. 360-362.

[4] D. Stern, Partners in Thought, (London: Routledge, 2009) p. 110ff.

of the mother.[5] This opens the way for us to God. When this process is damaged by abuse, the person's sense of self and worth does not develop - the opposite takes its place. We need the healing presence of a witness who will be with us as we tell our story - even when as in severe trauma we cannot always find the exact way to tell our story.

The practice of witnessing is sacred. By being present to the other we may facilitate the process of healing and the process of acceptance of one's self. Once the person is initiated it can lead from an interpersonal recognition to one that can be internalised by the person in pain. Acceptance is beginning to be internalised. As suffering is truly recognised, new images, symbols, words, narratives and meanings emerge in the context of a relationship that can be truly seen and known. Becoming accepting of oneself in one's wounds is the beginning of a new life, a new creation. When we look on the crucified and dead one we find we find this love. The light begins to come in, at first not very bright but in the power of God's Spirit the darkness is beginning to be overcome. There are people who can be with us in our experience of trauma and pain and they can mediate this light to us. The healing is not instant but it has begun. Unlike 'Rudy' of the song we have found people who recognise us.

One of the people who influenced Balthasar's interpersonal I-thou was Martin Buber who said: "Every particular Thou is a glimpse through to the eternal Thou". This is because man's "sense of Thou, which cannot be satiated, till he find the endless Thou, had the Thou present to it from the beginning."[6] (see Alan Lancashire, christendom-awake.org). God is always involved in our healing.

In the Gospel of John we read:

"Meanwhile, standing near the cross of Jesus were his mother, and his mother's sister, Mary the wife of Clopas,

---

[5] See H. Urs Von Balthasar, Love Alone is Credible (New York: Herder and Herder, 1969).

[6] Alan Lancashire, Influences on the Thought of Hans Urs Von Balthasar: Martin Buber and Karl Jaspers.

and Mary Magdalene. When Jesus saw his mother and the disciple whom he loved standing beside her, he said to his mother, "Woman, here is your son." Then he said to the disciple, "Here is your mother." And from that hour the disciple took her into his own home.

After this, when Jesus knew that all was now finished, he said (in order to fulfill the scripture), "I am thirsty." A jar full of sour wine was standing there. So they put a sponge full of the wine on a branch of hyssop and held it to his mouth. When Jesus had received the wine, he said, "It is finished." Then he bowed his head and gave up his spirit."

Jesus addresses his mother, Mary, as the 'woman' and the beloved disciple is not named. In ancient iconography the beloved discipled is painted as having both male and female characteristics. The beloved disciple can be male or female. Jesus asks the disciple and the woman (reminiscent of the woman in Genesis, see Gen 3:16) to be as one. Then he gave out (in Greek, *paradoken*) his spirit. "It is finished." (Jn 19:30). In his lonely journey into Hell the new community of Mary and the beloved disciple keep their prayerful vigil and God uses them to pray for him. After the resurrection Jesus and his new community of Mary and the beloved disciple continue their prayer for us in the Spirit. The whole scene is a drama we are called to enter. We can become the 'beloved disciple' and as Mary and the disciple accompanied Jesus in hell, so we can in union with her by the power of the Holy Spirit accompany the lonely Jesus who is found in so many of his brothers and sisters. The drama of Easter Saturday continues in time and will continue to the end of time.

Rabbi Menachem Mendel of Kotzk (+1859) said that "there is nothing as whole as a broken heart". This is paradoxical. When we receive a wound we are, as it were, driven out of Paradise. We no longer feel connected. We feel as though we are alone. Our broken heart is stranded and helpless. We wear masks in public to hide this from others. Others wear masks too to hide their broken hearts. It is only in the light of love and compassion that the pieces come together again. That is what we discover in Jesus and those who stood by his cross. Our brokenness opens us to the kindness of others.

Witness:

The term witness in English is the translation of the biblical Greek works martys, or martyr. There is a cost of listening - it means giving of oneself. It can also mean that we are put in touch with our own pain and need a witness to listen and be present to us. The ultimate witness is the lonely Jesus in Hell. It is to him that I have to return again and again. Only the wounded healer heals.

By giving ourselves to be witnesses we commit ourselves to a costly walking alongside those who suffer. This is something our culture runs from. It doesn't want to see, hear or acknowledge pain. It prefers to wear a mask. People suffer alone in hospitals, homes or in lonely flats. Denial doesn't make pain go away. There is a need for Easter Saturday people.

The good news of the Christian life is that this solidarity need not - and should not - be practiced alone. Jesus sent his disciples two by two. He commissioned the 'woman' and the 'one he loved' to be a new community in his Spirit. Nicholas Wolterstorff is an American philosopher. He lost his son and he felt an immense grief. He poured out is grief in the lament tradition of the Bible. He said:

> "If you think your task as comforter is to tell me that all things considered, it's not so bad, you do not sit with me in my grief but place yourself off in the distance away from me. Over there you are of no help. What I need to hear from you is how painful it is. I need to hear from you that you are with me in my desperation. To comfort me, you have to come close. Come sit with me on my mourning bench.
> [Lament for a Son (Grand Rapids: Eerdmans 1987) p. 34]

The life, death and resurrection of Jesus is a witness to a broken world. Jesus enters the brokenness to bring new life from the brokenness.

Sharing his life by the power of his Spirit brings us on a journey of healing.

We become new people 'in Christ'. He is the start of a new creation (2 Cor 5:17) and ultimately a new heaven and a new earth (Rev 21:1). 'In Christ' is a term used by Paul when we are in union with Christ.[7] Paul's use of the term in the Spirit (*en pneumati*) is closely related to being in Christ. Jesus died to embrace the broken and those caught in sinful alienation from God. "We are convinced that one has died for all; therefore all have died. And he died for all, that those who live might no longer live for themselves but for him who for their sake died and was raised." (2 Cor 5:14-15). Romans 14:7-8 speaks in the following terms: "None of us lives to himself and none of us dies to himself. If we live, we live to the Lord, and if we die we die to (Greek: *toi*) the Lord; therefore whether we live or die, we are the Lord's." Jesus becomes the pattern of our calling. This is what Paul means by 'in Christ'. This is when we are called to be witnesses.

There are times when we are not strong. First we have to "know with all the saints what is the length and width, height and depth of God's love" (Ephesians 3:18). To know the love of God which surpasses all knowledge we, again and again, have to be silent and keep company with the one who is more lonely and broken than we are and with him rise again to new life.

The Hope of God: (TDV, p. 181-191)

Charles Péguy was a French poet and essayist (+1914). He lost his faith but gradually returned. He wrote a famous poem, The Gate to the Mystery of the Second Virtue. He celebrates hope in the face of all that seems against that God's mercy which is the outpouring of his love will emerge as the final victor over all that is evil.

The poet begins with the paradoxical assertion that hope walks between its two big sisters, Faith and Charity, but it is she who actually leads

[7] see A. Oepke, article 'en', TDNT, II, p. 538f.

them (p. 534).[8] He goes on to tell the story of the woodcutter. He remembers that his children have been gravely ill. Then he hit upon the idea of putting them into the arms of the Mother of God. "After all you have countless others / what is one more or less" (p. 558). He brings his children with loving trust to the one "who has been given all the sorrow of the world / because the Son has taken all sin / but the mother has taken to herself all sadness" (ibid). She involves herself in our pain. Mary is called 'HOPE' "She who is only faith and love / because she is also hope made perfect." (p. 569).

Péguy speaks of hope in the heart of God "… He has unleashed fear and so has caused hope to well up / In the very heart of God / In the heart of Jesus" (p. 570). Anxiety and hope are simultaneously in the heart. Jesus is infinitely concerned about the one who is lost. This hope is "fragile, it depends on us whether the eternal voice will resound or lapse into silence" (p. 591-592). We are God's hope - broken and confused as we are, he has placed his hope in us that we bring his healing to the broken and lost. "We must place our hope in God since he has placed his in us" (p. 603).

The poet attributes something of the child's vitality to hope (on God's part or ours); for neither of them ultimately loses his way, despite fear, grief, anxiety or mortal danger (TDV, p. 187). He speaks of when the crown of thorns is being prepared that another crown is being woven for him, albeit invisibly. This crown is the crown of hope. This crown is entwined with "buds and leaves; gentle and fragrant, it refreshes his brow" (p. 598-602). Even though Jesus is broken yet his love never dies, and is sustained by his hope that his love will reach those who are in agony and need his compassion. Péguy admits in the poem: "We are capable of failing him", but "just as we, in our poor yet glorious churches, ring in the feast of Easter with our bells flying / God too rings out an eternal Easter for every soul that is saved / And says, 'After all, I wasn't mistaken: was I?'" (p. 617). God puts ultimate faith, love and hope in us. Many of us have learned not to love ourselves and yet the

---

[8] La Porche du mystère de la deuxième vertu (1911) in Oeuvres poétiques complêtêtes (Paris: Gallimard, 1957) p.527-670.

poem reminds us that God is never going to give up on us and when he wins our healing he is delighted. This is his joy.

At the end of the poem Péguy praises sleep. "The man who cannot sleep is failing to keep faith with hope" (p. 658). Sleep is shrouded in ultimate self-surrender to the Father. This is where we have to come in. We can feel the pain but it is in the surrender of oneself, one's faith, doubt, pain into the hands of God, in the face of all uncertainties to hope against hope. Self-surrender is ultimate; it is ultimate in God the Father, in the Son and in the Spirit, and it is ultimate in us too. (TDV, p. 188). "It is in dying that we are born to eternal life." (Peace prayer of St. Francis).

Chapter 5

Waiting for Godot:

In my life and the life there is also a hope - but a hope of what. After the night comes the day - yet when the night is darkest, then hope seems to deceive. In some lives people have ceased to hope and taken their lives - one of the great problems of today.

Music, art and writing have always been one of the great ways to express our loneliness and in doing so a sacred space, for me, is created. These are, for me, like hands raised in prayer.

Vincent Van Gogh (+1890) has always been one of my favourite artists. In his early years he attempted to be an evangelist in England. When he came to art he saw his work as another form of 'gospel' - he hoped his paintings would bring healing to those who beheld them. However he suffered from mental affliction all his life and spent long periods in profound alienation, isolation and loneliness. Yet from times of distress he produced works of extraordinary beauty that have become iconic. Towards the end of his life he felt profoundly lonely and felt he was a failure. He had failed in his attempt to make his work known, in his own mind. He caught this loneliness in his painting "Crows over the wheatfield". He painted this three days before he took his life. The ironic thing was critics were just beginning to take notice of his work. He wasn't a failure. People like me find great solace in his work. He creates a communion between artist and beholder and creates something beautiful. From the *tohu webohu*, the *temon* (see Gen 1:1-3) of his life he produced outstanding beauty.

Murphy:

Samuel Beckett (1906-1989) was an Irish avant-garde novelist, playwright, theatre director who spent most of his life in Paris. His works reflect a tragicomic outlook on human nature. Beckett studied

French, Italian and English at Trinity College, Dublin. He travelled, and lectured for a while. He began treatment with Dr. Wilfred Bion for his depression and anxiety. Bion was a psychoanalyst. His father died at this time. Beckett went to London and in 1935 began to work on his first novel *Murphy*. This work was published in 1938 and was not a great success. Most of the copies published were burned in the Blitz.

The plot of *Murphy* follows a man called Murphy who lives very much in his own head. His physical world is a run down apartment in West Brompton. The book begins with Murphy rocking back and forth in his rocking chair. Later on we are introduced to Celia Kelly, Murphy's lover, a prostitute and concerned friend. Murphy is urged by Celia to find a job and he begins work as a nurse in the Magdalen Mental Mercyseat in north London, finding the insanity of the patients an appealing alternative to conscious existence.

Murphy feels the world is hostile, offering him nothing. He has the experience of abandonment and absence. At its heart, Murphy suggests an early experience of disconnection from the good mother, her containing love and her joy with the infant.[1] Early experiences of maternal absence permeate the work's underlying emotional state, manifesting within Murphy as feelings of worthlessness, inadequacy and alienation. He is now a depleted, despairing self with a rage born out of neglect. In Murphy we see the narrative self of Murphy is attempting to restore a primal, maternal connection within itself, but Murphy fails and dies in an empty room which has a gas leak and explodes. We are left to guess as to whether Murphy meant to take his life or not.

The child that comes into the world has a need to love and be loved and the first object relationship is organised around this need. If the infant's need to love is rejected, it experiences the most painful emotional state: the feeling that it is unacceptable.[2] The experience of rejection of the

---

[1] see John Robert Keller, Samuel Beckett and the Primacy of Love (Manchester: Manchester University Press, 2002) p. 50.

[2] H. Guntrip: Schizoid Phenomena, Object Relations and the Self (London: Hogarth, 1968) p. 30.

infant is one that can deepen in severe trauma and is a pain (as we said) that comes back in many different guises. Those like Murphy who live in this state live in a frozen, loveless, world. I know that place. Reading Beckett helps to name it.

In Beckett's writing there is the sense of a depriving, uninterested world forming the person. There is a struggle between emergence and hiding, despair and hope, predicated on a sense that the world, being unknowable, may be as dangerous as it may be nurturing. (Keller, p. 36).

A Room Without a View[3]

Murphy's opening line "The sun shone, having no alternative, on the nothing new" (p. 1) reflects the closed, lifeless world of the narrator. He drifts into a 'blinding void' (p. 76) of lonely disconnection. The rocking chair is a secure, reliable object that never leaves him. It functions as the one thing that can soothe him by allowing momentary freedom from persecuting torments. Murphy rejects the world:

> "Somewhere a cuckoo-clock [...] became the echo of a street cry [...] These were sights and sounds that he did not like. They detained him in the world to which they belonged, but not he, as he fondly hoped.
> Slowly the world died down, the big world where [...] the light never waned the same way twice, in favour of the little [...] where he could love himself.
> Slowly, he felt better, astir in his mind, in the freedom of that light and dark that did not clash nor alternate, nor fade and lighten." (p. 57)

Life is a cursed undertaking. Murphy still seeks the best in himself (p. 71). Murphy's bad experiences at the Chandler confirms for him that the world is a painful, unloving world and this leads to his corresponding rage and depression.

---

[3] see S. Beckett, Murphy (New York: Grove Press, 1970).

Crying Over Cowjuice:

After leaving the Chandler, Murphy attempts to repair his damaged, internal world through a re-enactment of early nurturing. He decides against visiting a park, which would 'reek of death', or a return home which would disappoint Celia. He feels the only solution is to eat his lunch, 'more than an hour before he was due to salivate' (p. 79) a Pavlovian reference that reveals the mechanistic nature of his internal world. Lunch is a daily ritual and functions as a complex drama in which he enacts his internal struggles. To the outsider looking in this is an absurdity but to the confused and lonely these are attempts to make some connection with a world form which one feels alienated.

Seated in the restaurant, he begins to feel unreal, unloved: "The waitress stood before, with an air of such abstraction that he did not feel entitled to regard himself as an element in her situation" (p. 80). He goes to the park afterwards and sees a deformed woman, Miss Dew. She wanders in to feed the sheep who, too, wander into the park. Murphy had never seen such sheep, 'they all seemed one and all on the point of collapse' (p. 99-100). Murphy finds himself denying his own despair, as well as the anguish of the sheep, he devalues Miss Dew's attempts to feed the sheep. The sheep are Murphy. They reject Miss Dew's attempts to feed them like severely depressed infants do. Yet love is available for Murphy in the person of Celia but his inner world is held hostage by malevolent and attacking monsters, and this is despair in its coldest form. The world outside him is outside his control and will 'kick', mock and abandon him: in fantasy he yearns for a 'Supreme Caress' to soothe him and ease his pain.

Murphy begins work at the Asylum and finds a connection with a patient called Endon when he plays chess. Murphy has an intuitive understanding for the patients and particularly with Endon. When he is away from Endon he feels the absence like a small child; "facing the twelve hours of self, unredeemed self" (p. 188). The isolation seems unbearable, he feels disconnected and fragmented as the stars seem veiled by 'cloud or fog or mist' and the night sky appears dirty (p. 189).

He dreams of Celia, but is unable to overcome the life-destroying part of himself: 'the self whom he loved had the aspect [...] of real alienation. Or to put it perhaps more nicely: conferred that aspect to the self whom he hated' (p. 194). His night time separation from the patients becomes a time of increasing loneliness, since there was "no loathing to love from, no kick from the world that was not his, no illusion of caress from the world that might be" (p. 240). He misses the contact, failing to recognise that a 'caress' may be possible in the big world, just as the patients and Celia have a sense of his caress. Deep rejection as a child or the inner child of an older person can lead to this despair and fear that Murphy feels. Murphy in the end fails to make a connection with Endon.

> " 'the last at last seen of him
> himself unseen by him
> and of himself'
>
> A rest.
> 'The last Mr. Murphy saw of Mr. Endon was Mr. Murphy unseen by Mr. Endon. This was also the last Murphy saw of Murphy.'
> A rest.
> The relation between Mr. Murphy and Mr. Endon could not have been better summed up than by the former's sorrow at seeing himself in the latter's immunity from seeing anything but himself." (p. 249-50)

Murphy fails to make a loving attachment. He is now in desperation:

> "He saw the clenched fists and rigid upturned face of the Child in a Giovanni Bellini Circumcision, waiting to feel the knife. He saw eyeballs being scraped, first any eyeballs, then Mr. Endon's. He tried again with his father, his mother, Celia, Wylie, Neary, Cooper Miss Dew [...] with the men, women, children and animals that belong to even worse stories than this. In vain in all cases. He could not get a picture in his mind of any creature he had met, animal or human. Scraps of bodies, of landscapes, hands, eyes, lines and colours evoking nothing, rose and climbed out of sight

before him, as though reeled upward off a spool level with his throat." (p. 251-2)

He is terribly alone, rage having destroyed his inner world, and he attempts to assuage his disintegration by displacing his suffering into worse stories. He goes up to the garret to his rocking chair but there is an explosion in the gas system. Celia's world collapses too and the reader is left with a profound sense of loss. The world depicted by Beckett is the world those who have struggled with mental illness know. It is hard to make connections, one's inner world is shrouded in fear and pain and this leads to painful isolation which in turn leads to more pain. 'Murphy' and works like it help us to see our pain as in a mirror and this can help in the healing journey in coming to self. When we can recognize and name the unnameable then we know where we need healing. Sometimes naming the pain might be to call it 'Murphy' as Beckett did. Knowledge is power. Once we know what is wrong, we can focus and channel what we know to help us heal. We can begin to understand and accept ourselves.

Towards Godot:

After completing Murphy, Beckett travelled to Germany. He loved to attend art galleries. He wrote in his diary "the art that is a prayer sets up prayer, releases prayer in the onlooker, i.e., PRIEST: Lord have mercy upon us. PEOPLE: Christ have mercy upon us." I am always interested in how Beckett uses religious language to express himself. During this time he became conscious of the evils of Nazism. He also fell in love with a second cousin but this did not work out.

He became interested in the works of Dr. Johnson. He felt he had a soulmate in him. He too was interested in physical and mental illness, loneliness and decline, and obsessed with solitude and death. Beckett spoke of Johnson and noted his 'vile melancholy'; his 'aversion to merriment'; his 'peevishness of decay'; his fascination with lexicography and recondite words. Beckett had agreed to appear as a witness in a libel case that Harry Sinclair, a relative of Beckett, was bringing against Oliver St. John Gogarty. During the trial the defense counsel asked Beckett whether he would describe himself as a Christian, a Jew or an atheist to which Beckett replied "I am none of the three". Beckett did not like to be boxed into categories. As we saw, he could use and did use religious metaphors and language to embody his experiences. Some people blinked at this - but Beckett felt he did not want to be boxed in. During the trial Beckett was humiliated as a witness and it left him with a bitter taste. He liked the ordinary people of Ireland and the Irish countryside, but the society as it was then and represented in the libel case appalled him. He left Ireland, only returning for short periods afterwards.

He left for Paris. In 1938 he was the victim of a stabbing. James Joyce arranged for him to be treated privately. While in hospital he was visited by a Suzanne Dechevaux-Dumesnil. They became a couple and lived together for the rest of their lives. He would eventually marry Suzanne.

Then came the war. Beckett began work on his second novel Watt in 1941 but it was only after the war it would see light. Beckett felt the Nazis had to be opposed and joined the Resistance. His unit became known to the Germans and Beckett and Suzanne had to flee Paris. They escaped to Vichy France (the so-called independent part of France, even though it was under the Nazi's thumb). Beckett spoke little of his time with the Resistance but after the war De Gaulle awarded him the Croix de Guerre. He also received the 'Médaille de la Résistance'.

After the war Beckett returned to Dublin to visit his mother. She had failed enormously and Beckett was distressed to see this. He, too, had to be built up. During this time he had what he called a 'revelation' - again he was not afraid to use religious language. It has often been related to the 'vision' that Krapp experiences in Beckett's play "Krapp's Last Tape". Krapp's version is more dramatic than Beckett's experience with the wind howling and the waves crashing against the pier. The wild stormy night and the harbour setting of Krapp's fictional experience echo his romantic mystical experience with nature matching the excitement of his inner torment, revealing the truth to a man seeking his way. Beckett said he decided to write of the "things I feel". He decided to speak of the darkness of his inner world This darkness could extend to folly and failure, impotence and ignorance. The outer world would be filtered through his own imagination; inner desires and needs would be allowed a much greater freedom of expression; rational contradictions would be allowed in. His work would now focus on poverty, failure, exile and loss, on man as a 'non-knower' and as a 'non-can-er'. He became interested in the expression of Democritus that 'nothing is more real than nothing'. He decided now to write in French.

Beckett found it difficult to return to France. He joined the Irish Red Cross and worked at the Irish hospital in St. Lô. This had been the site of Allied bombing and was a wasteland. The wasteland would form the background for Godot. Eventually he and Suzanne would return to Paris and he began a new period of creative writing. From this time came the trilogy - Molloy, Malone Dies, and the Unnamable. He also turned to theatre and *En attendant Godot* (Waiting for Godot) was born. Initially the works were not well received but Suzanne went around Paris until she got his works published. 'Godot' premiered in Théatre de Babylone, directed by Roger Blin.

When Beckett was asked by Ralph Richardson if Godot meant God, Beckett replied "… if by Godot I had meant God I would have said God and not Godot".[4] Beckett also pointed out that he wrote in French. The French word for God is Dieu. However Beckett did concede later that there were often strong unconscious impulses that partly controlled his writing. He often spoke of being in a trance when he wrote.[5] Beckett himself began to wonder did he mean God after all. In the play two characters, Vladimir and Estragon, wait endlessly and in vain for the arrival of someone called Godot. This world is interrupted by the arrival of Pozzo and Lucky. The other character in the play is the 'boy' who informs Vladimir and Estragon that Mr. Godot cannot come. In a review

[4] quoted in J. Knowlson, Damned to Fame: The Life of Samuel Beckett, (London: Bloomsbury, 1996) p. 412.

[5] V. Mercier, Beckett/Beckett (London: Souvenir Press, 1990) p. 87.

in the "Irish Times" it was described as a play in which nothing happens - twice![6]

Waiting

The purpose of life is an unanswerable question. The world is utterly chaotic. According to the play a human being's life is totally dependent on chance, and by extension time is meaningless. A human being's life is also meaningless and the realisation of this drives humans to rely on nebulous, outside forces which may be real or not, for order and direction.

The idea of chance determining life is taken up by Vladimir who says: "One of the thieves was saved. It's a reasonable percentage". The idea of percentage is important because of its randomness. God, if he exists, contributes to the chaos by his silence. The very fact that God allows such an arbitrary system to continue makes him an accomplice.

The world of "Waiting for Godot" is one without any meaningful pattern, which symbolises chaos and confusion as the dominating forces in the world. There is no orderly sequence of events. A tree which was barren one day is covered with leaves in the next. The two tramps return to the same place every day to wait for Godot. No-one can remember exactly what happened the day before. The boy appears each day but the two tramps cannot remember him.

In Act 1 Pozzo is traveling to the market to sell Lucky, his slave. The next day in Act 2 Pozzo re-appears with Lucky but he is now blind and Lucky is mute. Pozzo has no recollection of the previous meeting and claims Lucky was always mute. Humans try to remain oblivious of their condition. Human beings cannot bear too much reality (Eliot). Vladimir and Estragon try to distract themselves from the endless wait by arguing over mundane topics, sleeping, chatting, and even contemplating suicide. They hope this will draw them close to the time when Godot comes - only he never comes.

[6] V. Mercier, The Irish Times, 18 February 1956, p. 6.

At the beginning of the second Act Vladimir begins to sing a song about the death of a day but the song never gets finished and he tries to start again - Act II ends with the lines

Vladimir: Well? Shall we go?
Estragon: Yes, let's go.

but the stage direction reads: They do not move. This circles back into Estragon's opening line in Act I, 'Nothing to be done', reflecting a verbal routine repeated several times wholly or in part.

Estragon: Let's go.
Vladimir: We can't.
Estragon: Why not?
Vladimir: We're waiting for Godot.
Estragon: Ah! (Pause: Despairing) What'll we do, what'll we do?
Vladimir: There's nothing we can do.[7]

When Pozzo and Lucky appear in Act 1, Pozzo is an imperious, pompous figure driving his slave Lucky along the road. When they leave Vladimir comments "Haven't they changed?" and insists "We know them, I tell you. You forget everything". (p. 48). In Act II Pozzo and Lucky appear again and Estragon has only a hazy memory of who they might be. The second happening (or non-happening) in Act 1 is the coming of the messenger boy to announce "Mr. Godot told me to tell you he won't come this evening but surely tomorrow" (p. 50). Vladimir says "I've seen you before, haven't I? It wasn't you came yesterday" while the boy responds this is his first time of coming (to which Vladimir responds 'words, words!'). The boy appears again in Act II with the same message. Vladimir again claims to recognise the boy but the boy denies it. Vladimir attempts to adjust to reality by saying perhaps it was the boy's brother who came the day before. 'I don't know', answers the boy. There is a sense of a total lack of a goal or an end.

[7] Samuel Beckett, Waiting for Godot (London: Faber and Faber, 1965) p. 68.

Godot is a mysterious figure, but the tramps are convinced if they are in the right place at the right time, he will show up. Vladimir says:

"What we are doing here, that is the question. And we are blessed in this, that we happen to know the answer. Yes, in the immense confusion one thing is clear. We are waiting for Godot to appear -
... We have kept our appointment, and that's an end to that. We are not saints but we have kept our appointment. How many people can boast as much?" (p. 80)

Estragon replies 'Billions' and Vladimir agrees. They are dislocated, out of rhythm and out of time. There is a pause here and Pozzo and Lucky reappear.

Beckett catches the mood that our waiting and our hope can be a futile exercise. When we look to Jesus and remember his parables of waiting (e.g. Lk 12:35-40), we are the people of the in-between. The future time of Jesus' coming is not-yet and we have to wait. In the waiting the pain can be heavy and in desperation we can think nothing will ever happen - the pain is permanent. Yet in the waiting there are moments of light, moments of grace, moments of the Spirit when things do not appear so bleak. Even in Godot there is the vaguest hint of that light. In the earliest stage directions of Beckett the scene is sparse and bare, but then as the play was produced, leaves appeared in the second scene - a mysterious allusion to hope, new birth. Christian hope is to hope against all hope. In another play of Beckett's 'Endgame' which came after 'Godot' there is a mysterious allusion to hope. The two characters of Endgame Clov and Hamm live in one room while outside is devastated by a nuclear holocaust. Then at the end of the play there is a boy who suddenly appears in view of the window, sitting on a rock when one had thought that the landscape was lifeless ("corpsed, all gone"). In the original French version the boy is related to the story of the resurrection, as the stone he sits on is conferred to the stage - the resurrection of Jesus, the one that was rolled away from the tomb. I see in Beckett's plays (Godot and Endgame) that there is a bleakness but from the bleakness new life is hinted at. Like Murphy (Beckett said the seeds of Godot can be found in Murphy) when our pain is diagnosed, the knowledge is power and we are on the road to self-acceptance. When we an accept ourselves then we can look at God who is love (1 Jn 4:16). We can begin to have the courage to accept we are accepted.

Godot became a worldwide success. In San Quentin a group of the inmates performed Godot - there was a stunned silence among the prisoners. They knew the dilemma, the pain of Vladimir and Estragon, the dissociation from time of the loneliness of waiting (waiting for what?). Beckett won the Nobel Prize for Literature in 1968 but he gave the money to the San Quentin group who were now free and had set up their theatre group. Beckett was constantly giving away money and precious items to help others.

Susan Sontag[8] tells the story of how in Sarajevo during the height of the Balkan crisis 'Godot' seemed as a light in the darkness for the people of Sarajevo. The city was under fire but Godot was performed every night. People from all over Sarajevo made their way to see the performance. Only one Act could be performed because the actors were too weak due to lack of food due to the siege of Sarajevo. The people related to the world of Vladimir and Estragon and they felt a catharsis in seeing their pain portrayed on the stage.

Both Murphy and Godot have that effect. When we cannot put words on our feelings, these provide a space where we can relate to the emotions of the characters. This has a cleansing, cathartic effect. I am left always after visiting these works with the feeling Beckett had before the paintings in Germany.

> Lord. Have mercy!
> Christ. Have mercy!
> Lord, Have mercy!

---

[8] Susan Sontag, Godot Comes to Sarajevo in The New York Review of Books, 21st Oct 1993.

Conclusion

The Beginning of a Healing Journey

In the 2013 film 'Gravity' Sandra Bullock's character Dr. Ryan Stone finds herself stranded in space with astronaut Matt Kowalski (played by George Clooney). In her desperation she feels the need to pray - but she realises she cannot because nobody taught her to pray. Her predicament is a common one. One of the great treasures of the Church is prayer and the teaching of countless witnesses on how to pray. Yet for all intents and purposes it is a treasure that is taken for granted and often forgotten. Now, more than ever, it is a treasure we must explore and share.

Sarah Coakley is an Anglican theologian and she is also a priest of the Church of England. She gave a talk online about her work.[1] In it she talks of her time as chaplain to a prison. One of the prisoners asked her to teach him and others how to pray silently. She had a large turnout and the prisoners really related to the experience and it gave many of them a feeling of esteem and sense of worth.

Beginning from experiences such as this she hopes to explore prayer and its effects in her Systematic Theology of which 'God, Sexuality and the Self' is the first volume. She also draws attention to Romans 8:26f where St. Paul tells us:

> "Likewise the Spirit helps us in our weakness; for we do not know how to pray as we ought, but that very Spirit intercedes with sighs too deep for words. And God, who searches the heart, knows what is in the mind of the Spirit because the Spirit intercedes for the Saints according to the will of God."

---

[1] I found the talk at St. John's Nottingham website. She spoke about her book: God, Sexuality and the Self (Cambridge: Cambridge University Press, 2013)

We are not alone when we pray. The presence of the Spirit shows us that if we begin he will bring our prayer to completion. I remember a friend of mine who was in anguish. He told me he could not pray, but when he felt really low he held on to a cross he had. I told him that the effort to pray is prayer and I told him about this part in St. Paul. The Spirit is in his prayers and directs it to the mind of God. Prayer is not a magical cure-all: Yet by praying in silence in the presence and Spirit of the wounded Jesus we begin to allow the light to come through and dispel the darkness. It is not instant but it is the beginning of a healing journey.

St. John of the Cross tells us that "the Living Flame of Love" is the Holy Spirit. He is the flame of divine love (Living Flame, 1:19). It is he who wounds the soul in order to dispose it for divine union and transformation - "just as the fire that penetrates a log of wood is the same that first makes an assault on the wood, wounding it with the flame, drying it out and stripping it of its unsightly qualities until it is so disposed that it can be penetrated and transformed into the fire" (Living Flame, 1:19 see also 2:7).

When we pray silently we begin to learn many things about ourselves. As victims of abuse people can find there is much self-hatred and hurt. The prospect of staying silent can be overwhelming and the temptation is to run and be busy - in the end the pain does not go away. Yet in becoming aware of what is inside us John tells us that the Spirit is healing us of these memories until we come to be one with the fire, the fire of love. It is from this perspective that we can get the courage to pray and learn that we are accepted and loved. As time goes by we learn to internalise this and thus begin a journey of healing.

Thinking About the Holy Spirit

I began this journey reflecting on the Holy Spirit using Von Balthasar's ideas. This was to lead us to Christ and his lonely journey of Holy Saturday. However the Spirit does not allow any one interpretation to define him. The Book of Genesis has much to teach us about the action of the Spirit. The NRSV begins with these lines:

"In the beginning when God created the heavens and the earth, the earth was a formless void and darkness covered the face of the deep while a wind from God swept over the waters." (Gen 1:1-3)

Federico Giuntoli[2] analyses the text of Genesis. He looks at the Hebrew word *'bereshit'* and the word for creates *'bara'*. He suggests a better translation of the first sentence of Genesis would be "When God began to create the heavens and the earth..." Creation takes place over the chaos of *'tohu webohu'*. The deep or abyss is called *'tehom'*. It is from this primordial chaos that God creates. Giuntoli's translation shows that creation is not just a once off. God's creation is continual and the resurrection of Jesus shows us a new creation to which we are called. The Spirit is called the breath of God. It is new life. This breath of God, the Spirit, is the means by which God creates. In our own hearts are these energies of confusion and chaos, the *'tohu webohu'* and the *'tehom'*. Over our weakness and brokenness the Spirit hovers to create us anew. The Spirit in Hebrew is the *'ruach'* of God.

There is much more that can be said of the Spirit but for our purposes I go to St. Paul in his Letter to the Romans. In it he tells us: "For all who are led by the Spirit of God are the children of God" (8:14). The baptised person has the Spirit of God dwelling in him or her. Paul intermingles the terms 'Spirit of God' and 'Spirit of Christ' in his writings. The Spirit is the source of life and vitality. The Spirit not only gives life but establishes us as children of God. This is our supreme dignity. We are in a special relationship with Jesus, the unique Son of God and his Father. This enables us to cry out: "Abba! Father." (Rom 8:15 see Gal 4:6). "It is that very Spirit bearing witness with our Spirit that we are children of God, and if children then heirs, heirs of God and joint heirs with Christ - if in fact we suffer with him so that we may also be glorified with him." (8:15-17). Our sufferings are Christ's. In the context of this work our Holy Saturday experience is his. We share the pain now with him so that we can come to a new day of life.

---

[2] F. Giuntoli, Genesis I-II (Saint Pauls Publications, Milan, 2013) p. 72-77.

Paul goes on to say: "I consider the sufferings of this present time are not worth comparing with the glory that is to be revealed to us" (Rom 8:18). We, in the in-between time, have to accept this in faith. We have to have courage and accept that we are accepted. In the face of all that is negative, it really does take courage. Paul tells after this that our pain is part of the groaning of all creation (Rom 8:19-25). Our hope "is for what we do not see, we wait for it with patience" (Rom 8:25). Our hope is in Jesus who suffered hell and was born into eternal life.

Then Paul gives us the lines

"Likewise the Spirit helps us in our weakness; for we do not know how to pray as we ought but that very Spirit intercedes for us with sighs too deep for words. And God, who searches the heart, knows what is in the mind of the Spirit because the Spirit intercedes for the Saints according to the will of God." (Rom 8:26-27)

We do not know how to pray perfectly, but the part that the Spirit prays in us removes our need to be perfect. He fills out what is lacking in our prayer. The Spirit searches the heart. This is an Old Testament name for God (1 Sam 16:7; 1 Kgs 8:39: Pss 7:11; 17:3; 139:1). Only God himself knows the language and mind of the Spirit. Our role is to place ourselves before God and abandon ourselves through the Holy Spirit into his hands. We are not alone and we find God is in each of us to hold us and make us new. In this light even if things seem to go wrong yet "we know that all things work for good for those who love God, who are called according to his purpose" (Rom 8:28). Thérèse lived this 'abandon' radically and allowed God work through her.

Paul concludes this chapter with an act of faith "For I am convinced that neither death, nor life, nor angels, nor rulers, nor things present, nor things to come, nor powers, nor height, nor depth, nor anything else in all creation, will be able to separate us from the love of God in Christ Jesus our Lord" (Rom 8:38f). The love of God is the very centre of God - he will never withdraw. Jesus was driven to the depths of hell but he never withdrew his love. This love proved stronger than death.

We have to learn and relearn to place ourselves before this Jesus. The Spirit is with us. We have to have the courage to accept acceptance. Our experience of rejection can be so strong that this becomes too frightening - yet we find ourselves again in the presence of the loneliest one, Jesus in hell. He suffered this so that we might know we are not alone. He shows us he loves us, and accepts us. He is prepared to become the loneliest one who ever walked among us so that we might know that God is with us. In the silence of prayer we must begin and begin again and again.

Bibliography

Samuel Beckett, *Murphy*, New York, 1970.

Samuel Beckett, *Waiting for Godot*, London 1965.

Jennifer Beste, *God and the Victim: Traumatic Intrusions in Grace and Freedom*, New York, 2007.

Cathy Caruth, *Unclaimed Experience: Trauma, Narrative, and History*, John Hopkins Un., 1996.

– *Literature in the Ashes of History*, Baltimore, 2013.

Cathy Caruth, ed., *Trauma: Explorations in Memory*, Baltimore, 1995.

Sarah Coakley, *God, Sexuality and the Self*, Cambridge, 2013.

Fydor Dostoyevsky, *The Idiot*, London 1992.

Wendy Farley, *Tragic Vision and Divine Compassion*, Louisville, 1990.

Sigmund Freud, *Beyond the Pleasure Principle*, New York, 1961.

Federico Giuntoli, *Genesi I-II*, Milan, 2013.

Nicholas Healy, *The Eschatology of Hans Urs Von Balthasar*, Oxford, 2005.

Judith Herman, *Complex PTSD in Psychotraumatology*, ed. George S. Everly, Jeffrey Lating, New York: 1995, p. 87-102.

Judith Herman, *Trauma and Recovery*, New York, 1992.

Abraham Heschel, *The Prophets*, New York, 1955.

Anne Hunt, *The Trinity and the Paschal Mystery*, Collegeville, 1997.

John Robert Keller, *Samuel Beckett and the Primacy of Love*, Manchester, 2002.

James Knowlson, *Damned to Fame: The Life of Samuel Beckett*, London, 1996.

David Lauber, *Barth and the Descent into Hell*, Aldershot, 2004.

Andrew Louth, *The Place of the "Heart of the World" in the Theology of Hans Urs Von Balthasar*, in The Analogy of Beauty, ed. John Riches, Edinburgh, 1986.

Vivian Mercer, *Beckett/Beckett*, London, 1990.

Bonnie J. Miller-McElmore, *Suffering* in the Blackwell Companion to Practical Theology, ed. B. J. Miller-McElmore, Oxford, 2012.

A. Oepke, *'en'* TDNT, II, p. 538f.

Charles Péguy, *La Porche du Mystère de la deuxième vertu*, 1911, in Oeuvres Poétiques complêtes, Paris, 1957, p. 527-670.

Shelly Rambo, *Spirit and Trauma*, Louisville, 2010.

D. Stern, *Partners in Thought*, London, 2009.

Supertramp, *'Rudy'*, from the album *Crime of the Century*, 1974.

Supertramp, *Even in the Quietest Moments*, from the album *Even in the Quietest Moments*, 1977.

The Who, *Quadrophenia*, 1973 rock opera.

Hans Urs Von Balthasar, *The Unknown Lying Beyond the Word* in Explorations in Theology III, Creator Spirit, p. 105-117.

  – *The Holy Spirit as Love*, Explorations in Theology III, Creator Spirit, p. 117-135.

Hans Urs Von Balthasar, *First Glance at Adrienne Von Speyr*, San Francisco, 1981.

Hans Urs Von Balthasar, *Heart of the World*, San Francisco, 1979.

Hans Urs Von Balthasar, *Plus Loin que la Mort*, Communio no. VI, 1 – 1981, p. 2-5.

Hans Urs Von Balthasar, *You Crown the Year*, San Francisco, 1989.

Hans Urs Von Balthasar, *Love Alone is Credible*, New York, 1969.

Hans Urs Von Balthasar, *Theological Aesthetics*, 7 vols, T. & T. Clark, 1982-1989 (GL in the text).

– *Theodrama*, 5 vols, T. & T. Clark, 1990-1998 (TD in text).

– *Theologic*, 3 vols, T. & T. Clark, 2000-2005 (TL in text).

Hans Urs Von Balthasar, *Mysterium Paschale*, Grand Rapids, 1993.

Hans Urs Von Balthasar, *Explorations in Theology III, Creator Spirit*, San Francisco, 1993.

B. A. Van Der Kolk, A. C. McFarlane, and Lars Weiseth, eds., *Traumatic Stress: The Effects of Overwhelming Experience on Mind, Body and Society*, New York, 1996.

Basil Van Der Kolk in *Traumatic Stress*, p. 3-23, 214-241, 182-213, 417-440.

Adrienne Von Speyr, *Kreuz und Hölle, 1*, Einsiedeln, 1966.

– *Kreuz und Hölle, II*, Einsiedeln, 1972.

Jeffrey A. Vogel, *The Unselfing Activity of the Holy Spirit in the Theology of Hans Urs Von Balthasar*, in Logos, vol 10, 2007.

Nicholas Walterstorff, *Lament for a Son*, Grand Rapids, 1987.

Simone Weil, *Waiting for God*, London, 2001.

59067833R00042

Made in the USA
Charleston, SC
26 July 2016